Church and World

Church and World
Eusebius's, Augustine's, and Yoder's Interpretations of the Constantinian Shift

Simon P. Schmidt

James Clarke & Co

James Clarke & Co
P.O. Box 60
Cambridge
CB1 2NT
United Kingdom

www.jamesclarke.co
publishing@jamesclarke.co

Paperback ISBN: 978 0 227 17725 9
PDF ISBN: 978 0 227 90726 9

British Library Cataloguing in Publication Data
A record is available from the British Library

First published by James Clarke & Co, 2020

Copyright © Wipf and Stock Publishers, 2019

Published by arrangement
with Pickwick Publications

All rights reserved. No part of this edition may be reproduced, stored electronically or in any retrieval system, or transmitted in any form or by any means, electronic, mechanical, photocopying, recording, or otherwise, without prior written permission from the Publisher (permissions@jamesclarke.co).

This book is dedicated to my four godsons:
Julius, Karl, Poul, and Vilhelm.

Contents

Preface   xi
Abbreviations   xiv

Part I: The Constantinian Shift—An Introduction

1. History and Theology   3
   1.1 Problem   3
   1.2 Material   8
   1.3 Methodology   13
   1.4 Structure   21

Part II: An Early Interpretation

2. Eusebius of Caesarea   25
   2.1 Introduction   25
   2.2 Constantine   26
      2.2.1 Constantine and His Time   26
      2.2.2 Constantine the Emperor   27
      2.2.3 Constantine and the Church   28
   2.3 Eusebius   29
      2.3.1 Eusebius as Historian and Theologian   29
      2.3.2 Eusebius as a Theological Historian   29
      2.3.3 The Genre of the *Vita Constantini*   31
   2.4 Eusebius's Interpretation of the Constantinian Shift   32
      2.4.1 Church and Empire   34
         2.4.1.1 The State Taking Over the Church or the Church Taking Over the State?   34
         2.4.1.2 The Common Good   35
      2.4.2 Church and Emperor   37
         2.4.2.1 The Relationship between the Church and the Emperor   37

            2.4.2.2 The Special Relationship between the Emperor and
                God   39
            2.4.2.3 The Personal Piety of the Emperor   41
            2.4.2.4 The Emperor's Embrace of Christianity   44
            2.4.2.5 Violence Committed by the Emperor   46
        2.4.3 Theology and Politics   49
            2.4.3.1 The Christian Mission   49
            2.4.3.2 God in Control of the Course of History   51
            2.4.3.3 Baptism and Funeral   52
    2.5 The Contemporary Debate   55
        2.5.1 A Renewed Interest in Eusebius   55
        2.5.2 Theological History-Writing   58
    2.6 Conclusion   59

Part III: A Corrective

3. Augustine of Hippo   65
    3.1 Introduction   65
    3.2 Augustine and Eusebius (Exterior Differences)   66
        3.2.1 Different Time   67
        3.2.2 Different Location   69
    3.3 Augustine's Interpretation of the Constantinian Shift   69
        3.3.1 Book 19   73
        3.3.2 Two Households   74
        3.3.3 The Concept of Two Households and Loyalty toward the
            Empire   76
        3.3.4 The Constantinian Shift and the Theory of Just War   78
        3.3.5 Conclusion   80
    3.4 The Contemporary Debate   82
        3.4.1 Robert Markus's Concept of the Secular   82
        3.4.2 Oliver O'Donovan's Critique   83
    3.5 Augustine and Eusebius (Internal Differences)   87
        3.5.1 Different Theological Sources   87
        3.5.2 The Purpose of Writing a Historical Account   90
        3.5.3 Different Conception of the Progression of History   91
        3.5.4 Different Theological Framework   93
    3.6 Conclusion   94

Part IV: A Current Interpretation

4. John Howard Yoder   99

4.1 Introduction   99
      4.1.1 Yoder as Theologian and Historian   100
      4.1.2 Yoder as a Mennonite Historian   104
   4.2 Yoder's Interpretation of the Constantinian Shift   107
      4.2.1 Three Essays in Outline   107
         4.2.1.1 "The Constantinian Sources of Western Social Ethics"   107
         4.2.1.2 "The Meaning of the Constantinian Shift"   108
         4.2.1.3 "Peace Without Eschatology"   109
      4.2.2 The Constantinian Shift and Its Theological Consequences   110
      4.2.3 The Constantinian Shift and Theological Authority   114
      4.2.4 The Constantinian Shift and the Understanding of Ecclesiology   117
      4.2.5 The Constantinian Shift and the Understanding of Eschatology   119
      4.2.6 The Constantinian Shift and the Emergence of the Theory of Just War   120
      4.2.7 The Constantinian Shift and the Church as Mainstream Culture   123
      4.2.8 The Constantinian Shift and the Contemporary Situation of the Church   124
      4.2.9 Conclusion   127
   4.3 The Contemporary Debate   129
      4.3.1 Criticism of Yoder's Historical Analysis   130
      4.3.2 Criticism of Yoder's Theological Analysis   136
   4.4 Yoder and the Ancient Interpretations   139
      4.4.1 The Church in the World   141
      4.4.2 The Church and War   144
      4.4.3 The Church and Eschatology   146
   4.5 Conclusion   147

Part V: Perspectives

5. Church, History and Theology   153
   5.1 Three Interpretations of the Place of the Church in the World   154
   5.2 The Validity of Theological History-Writing   155
   5.3 A Way Forward for the Church   157
Bibliography 161

4.1 Introduction — 99
4.1.1 Yoder as Theologian and Historian — 100
4.1.2 Yoder as a Mennonite Historian — 104

Preface

"In the world but not of the world." It is a complex expression. Does it imply Christians ought not to enjoy the physical nature of being created and should instead wait out their time on earth until they are whisked away to some celestial realm? At certain times, it has been interpreted as such in the Christian tradition. As a Lutheran, however, I hold it to be a freeing message that tradition can occasionally be wrong; that God is greater than the church is able to comprehend.

There is, namely, another way to interpret it. Not as an expression of skepticism towards the physical nature of creation but rather as a statement in regard to the world-order. It can be construed as an assertion that Christians belong to a community, in which the story of this world is interpreted differently; a community that does not view the basic relationship between human beings as that of competition. Rather, Christians are in this world order, but do not have to play by its rules. Not because Christians think themselves too pure or too good to play along. But simply because if just a fraction of that story about God's son coming into this world, dying and becoming alive again, really happens to be true, then all the fighting and competing, characteristic of late-capitalist societies, really does appear quite foolish.[1]

That is one way of interpreting what it means to be in the world but not of the world. In a Western society, where the church is again slowly moving away from the center of society and has to understand itself as one community among many others, questions pertaining to the role of the church in society are becoming more pressing. With the publication of the much debated *The Benedict Option: A Strategy for Christians in a Post-Christian*

---

1. For the biblical passages that have provided scriptural basis for the expression "in the world but not of the world," see Rom 12:2 and John 17:14–16. It is interesting to note how Paul uses αἰών while John uses κόσμος. The first being closer to meaning "world order," the second closer to "creation."

Preface

Nation in 2017 these questions were, once again, on the minds of many in the church, especially in the United States. That said, it is not the first time the church has had to find its place in an ever-changing context. The discussion surrounding how the church should understand its role in relation to the society it finds itself in, has been going on for a long time. As with many other theological conversations, this is one that takes place across borders and across centuries.

By focusing on the specific question of how to interpret the Constantinian shift, this book identifies the theological assumptions, which come to determine how the role of the church in the world is perceived. Attention to these theological assumptions qualifies and provides nuances to the current debate. This book does not provide the answer to the question "how should we think about the role of the church in contemporary Western society?" However, by examining how the question has been answered at three junctures in the history of the church, hopefully it will provide a lay of the land; a map of the territory to be navigated.

The first edition of this text was written as a so-called "prize-essay" at the University of Copenhagen, Denmark. As has been the norm in Lutheran Scandinavia, Denmark still has an established church, there is a secretary for ecclesial affairs and the queen is the head of the church. However, while writing this paper I was located in the United States, with its sprawling multitude of unregulated Christian churches. Thus, the very birth of this book took place at a point of tension between different views on the church in the world. Such a conflicted birth has not led, at first, to a strong opinion on how things are to be. Instead, it has led to an initial inquiry and a reflection on the many different situations the church has found and still finds itself in.

Such a position of questioning is vulnerable. A position of vulnerability can only be sustained if there are people around, who are willing to help and listen; when one asks questions about what it is to be a human being and what it is to be a Christian. Here, churches, family, teachers, advisers, and good friends have all played an important role. Thank you.

Furthermore, in particular situations, unlikely communities arise. I had the privilege of using the well-equipped Duke Divinity School Library throughout the greater part of the writing process. Here, a bond formed for a little while between three people: Arthurine, who was studying for her medical school examinations, Doron, who was finishing his PhD, and me. In the daily work of reading, writing, and eating together, a special

Preface

community arose, of people from all over the world with different backgrounds and very different projects. It is in extreme situations, when we find ourselves in foreign lands, that a way out of no way is opened up.

                The Black Diamond, Copenhagen, July 2018.

Abbreviations

VC: *Vita Constantini*
ciu.: *De Civitate Dei*
NRSV: New Revised Standard Version

Part I

The Constantinian Shift—

An Introduction

1
History and Theology

1.1 Problem

How to be "in the world but not of the world" is a classic theological question. The tension in the question is related to two models of the good life laid out in the Christian Scriptures. Is the good life modeled in the stories of the patriarchs, living in accordance with this world order and dying as octogenarians surrounded by goats and grandchildren? Or is the good life modeled in the stories of the prophets and Christ, speaking out against the wrongs of this world order and dying as a martyr at age thirty-three? These two models of the good life can both be found in OT and NT, but are not immediately reconcilable. Nevertheless, Christians throughout the ages have had to live their lives in tension between these two models. Christians have had to answer this question of how to be in this world on an individual level, applying it to their own life. But also on a communal level, with respect to how the church is to exist and organize, they have had to contemplate the question of how to be in the world without being of the world. A lot of Protestant theological consideration has gone into answering the question on an individual level, but much less consideration has gone into answering it on a communal level. In particular Lutheran theologians have not considered the question of how to be "in the world but not of the world" along the lines of an ecclesiological question.[1]

---

1. It is remarkable how the Lutheran Church has been able to foster theologians who were profoundly imaginative in formulating groundbreaking new theologies dealing with the relationship between the single individual and God. But when it came to the

Church and World

No universal answer can be given to the question of how to be in the world without being of the world, as it is a question, both on the individual and the communal level, heavily dependent of the context. The question of how to be in the world without being of the world on a communal level can, with precaution, take the form of the question of the relationship between the church and the state.[2] How the church is to relate to the state is a question that likewise will have to take into account the historical setting of the church and can thus never be answered in a one-time, abstract manner. Stanley L. Greenslade expressed this succinctly in 1953, when he gave the F. D. Maurice lectures at King's College London under the heading *Church and State from Constantine to Theodosius*. Greenslade states that one must "recognize the difficulty of finding any pattern of Church and State relations which shall conform to luminously clear Christian principles."[3] Also when posed as pertaining to the relationship between church and state, the theological question of how to be in the world but not of the world cannot be answered in a definitive normative way, as it would disregard the context in which that question is posed. However, what can be accomplished, in terms of a general approach to the question, is to gain a better understanding of what is at stake theologically and historically. And gaining an understanding of the nuances in a question constitutes the first step in approaching an answer. Thus, to achieve a better understanding of what is at stake theologically in the question of how the church is to be in the world without being of the world is the modest aspiration for this book.

One way of achieving such an understanding is to look into what theologians at various times have thought about this question. Though these theologians might well be situated in vastly different contexts, an investigation of different interpretations of how the church is to be in the

---

communal part of the Christian existence, the church and the body and its relationship to other bodies, their imagination has fallen surprisingly short, and they have tended to affirm the existing order of society. Martin Luther (1483–1546) is of course an example, but also Søren Kierkegaard (1813–1855) and his strong support of the Absolute Monarchy falls into this pattern. The reasons for this characteristic of Lutheran theology cannot be thoroughly investigated in this book, but throughout we will be able to identify some theological patterns for why it came to be so. For now it will suffice to say that it is probably no coincidence that it was N. F. S. Grundtvig (1783–1872)—who drew much inspiration from the early church—who is the exception in Danish theology to the rule of Lutheran theologians not prioritizing ecclesiology.

2. "The world" and "the state" are not equivalent terms, but within ecclesiology the state can take the place as the other, which the church has to relate to.

3. Greenslade, *Church and State from Constantine to Theodosius*, 81–82.

world will contribute to a better understanding of the question in general. As it is difficult to analyze such a foundational matter in itself, a certain entry point needs to be identified. One such entry point is an analysis of how the Constantinian shift is interpreted in three paradigmatic works. Such a focused question provides a perspective necessary to yield meaningful insights pertaining to the abstract question of the relationship between church and world. An investigation of the historiography of the Constantinian shift will hence serve as a way to gain knowledge of how to think about these matters historically and theologically.

By analyzing paradigmatic interpretations of the Constantinian shift, two insights will hopefully be achieved. The first insight illumines how interpretations of the Constantinian shift through the history of the church has been influenced by theological underpinnings. As a result of this a second insight will illumine overarching theological issues at stake in the question of the relationship between church and state.[4]

After an account of the research question, I will here move on to provide a necessary account of two key terms and then provide a short outline of the book, thus enabling us to begin the investigation.

A question pertaining to historiography, such as the one that has occasioned this book, could be answered in a short-ranging manner. Such a book might consist in a detailed analysis of how, for example, Eusebius of Caesarea (ca. 260–339) and Lactantius (ca. 250–325) depicted and interpreted the Constantinian shift. It could be supplemented with a discussion of how scholarly literature, within the last thirty years or so, has reevaluated Eusebius's works. A book like that would surely prove interesting. But such a narrow investigation would not provide the insights into the foundational theological underpinnings that influenced the interpretation of a historical event like the Constantinian shift. To understand what has formed the historiography of the Constantinian shift it is necessary to get to the theological presuppositions of the theologians who interpreted it. These are theological presuppositions pertaining to ecclesiology, ethics and eschatology.

---

4. Obviously, the Constantinian shift is not the only juncture in history at which the relationship between church and empire or state was being renegotiated. The Carolingian King Pepin's alliance with the church in 752, the Investiture Controversy in the eleventh and twelfth centuries, Pope Boniface VIII's *Unam Sanctam* from 1302, the Reformation history of the sixteenth and seventeenth centuries, the Catholic Church in France during the Enlightenment in the seventeenth and eighteenth centuries are examples of other more or less viable entry points into this complex of problems.

Church and World

Church history is a theological discipline that takes into account both how the interpretation of history will have a theological aspect to it as well as how the interpretation of history can be informed by theological presuppositions. This book takes a theological approach, as it is precisely at this point church history has something distinct to offer the wider academic field of history.[5]

How theology can contribute to the wider academy is one of the questions I will touch on when I below will be looking into the theoretical and methodological framework for this book. Why have I chosen to look at interpretations of the Constantinian shift as expressed by three theologians? What material will I be looking at and why has it been chosen? How will I approach the analysis of this material?

Prior to Constantine's (ca. 272–337) so-called *Edict of Milan* (313) the Emperor Diocletian's persecutions of Christians had made it potentially lethal to be a Christian in parts of the Roman Empire,[6] whereas the Emperor Theodosius in 380 made it potentially lethal not to be a Christian in the Roman Empire.[7] During a short period of time, Christianity went from being one religion among many to being the only allowed religion.[8] This made it necessary for the church to reconsider a whole range of questions. What is the relationship between church and the empire? How does a proper church service look like? What is good government? Is God in control of the course of political history?

---

5. With that being said, the new scholarly interest among classicists in Eusebius will indeed serve as an auxiliary resource for this book.

6. The title *Edict of Milan* is problematic. Timothy Barnes states that "there is no ancient evidence whatever that either Constantine and Licinius jointly or Constantine alone issued any edict or general law respecting Christianity either during or immediately after their meeting in Milan." See Barnes, *Constantine*, 95. But the term does reveal how Constantine has been portrayed, though not in full accord with the historical facts. A portrayal which, according to Barnes, has served "to blind modern historians of Constantine to the fact that Gallienus legalized Christianity more than a dozen years before the first Christian emperor was born." See Barnes, *Constantine*, 97. Gallienus (218–268) was tolerant toward Christians as part of instigating a larger religious renaissance.

7. Technically Galerius's (not to be confused with Gallienus) *Edict of Toleration* from 311 meant the official end to most Christian persecution, but only in 313 did Christianity officially gain the status of a *religio licita*.

8. Such categorical depictions of historical developments presented in this introductory section are obviously bound to be an oversimplification of the nuanced relationship between the church and the Roman Empire in the fourth century and later on. It does convey a valid message, though, of a general trend.

History and Theology

Only since the Enlightenment has this union between the church and the state, founded in the fourth century, started to be partly broken up institutionally and intellectually, thereby once again raising a number of questions of how the church is to be in the world.[9]

As we will see throughout the book, there seems to be some similarity between the situation in the fourth-century Roman Empire and the contemporary situation in the West, in regard to a multi-religious environment. Such an environment spurs new questions in theology and did both in the fourth century and in contemporary time lead to new interpretations of the Constantinian shift and its consequences. Within contemporary Anglo-Saxon ecclesiology the questions of how to be the church in a post-Christendom context has come to expression in considerations on how to situate the church in this new landscape in the West.[10] But such questions are not new. It is not the first time the church has to be the church in a situation, where questions of the relationship to wider society are being renegotiated. To look at how theologians at earlier ages have interpreted the role of the church in a pluralist context will prove helpful for grappling with such issues today. Not necessarily to come up with distinct answers, but rather to gain a better understanding of the question. This book is bringing together perspectives from church history, ecclesiology and political theology in order to shed light on what is at stake theologically in the question of the Constantinian shift.[11]

---

9. The two terms "empire" and "state" are used here somewhat synonymously, though it must be acknowledged how the societal structures in which the church found itself in the fourth century were very different from the societal structures in later Western Europe; not least the understanding of the role of religion in public and politics had changed.

10. The British theologian Lesslie Newbigin's *Gospel in a Pluralist Society* (1989) is one of the important works to have initiated such a post-Christendom conversation in contemporary ecclesiology, whereas David Bosch's *Transforming Mission* (1991) opened the debate within the field of missiology. For a recent engagement with these questions in a Scandinavian context, see Jeppe Bach Nikolajsen, *Distinctive Identity of the Church*; see also Jeppe Bach Nikolajsen, "Missional Folk Church?," 23–36.

11. By "political theology" I do not mean to denote a form of political theology according to which theology is utilized to further some political (often Marxist) goal; i.e., making theology based on an already stated politic goal. I use the term to denote a theology that is carried out with the understanding that theology will necessary have a political side to it due to the all-embracing character of its subject matter. As Oliver O'Donovan puts it: "Rule out the political questions and you cut short the proclamations of God's saving power." See O'Donovan, *Desire of the Nations*, 3. O'Donovan argues that the theopolitical character of most theology has been occluded in the shadow of the

To restrict this book to dealing only with the narrowly historical aspects of the Constantinian shift would ignore the theological perspectives. But these perspectives are necessary in order to understand properly how an account of history and an account of theology come together in the examined interpretations of the Constantinian shift. The question of the interpretation of the Constantinian shift is a battleground, in which different theological presuppositions encounter each other. It is a question of contention, where the notions a theologian holds in regard to such dogmas as creation, ecclesiology, sanctification and eschatology are revealed—the three interpretations of the Constantinian shift we will look at in this book are no exception. I will now turn to identify texts where this battle is waged.

1.2 Material

In this book I will be analyzing texts. Here I will provide an account of which texts will be analyzed, account for why they have been chosen, and provide a short ecumenical argument for the legitimacy of bringing texts from such different place and time into conversation.

In this book I will not attempt a general analysis of the historiography of the Constantinian shift as expressed throughout all of church history. Instead I will narrow the focus down to three authors, as this will allow me to investigate main paradigmatic stances in the interpretation of the Constantinian shift. I will narrow it further down, though, as I will not attempt to give an account of the historiography of the Constantinian shift as expressed in three complete authorships. Instead, I will analyze how an interpretation of the Constantinian shift comes to expression in three corpora of text. By focusing closely on three different interpretations of the Constantinian shift, main historical and theological postures will be exposed, which would not have become clear had a strictly historiographical reading been chosen. An analysis of such a narrowly defined material will provide a sustained engagement with the various positions and thereby enable us to further understand what is at stake in the interpretation of the Constantinian shift.

---

modern period. He recounts how the ignorance of the Old Testament combined with the fear of the influence of religion on politics after the Enlightenment let to theology gradually losing its political voice. See O'Donovan, *Desire of the Nations*, 1–120.

Vita Constantini (*VC*) by Eusebius of Caesarea (ca. 260–339), *De Civitate Dei* (*ciu.*)[12] by Augustine of Hippo (354–430), and the three essays "The Constantinian Sources of Western Social Ethics," "The Meaning of the Constantinian shift," and "Peace Without Eschatology" by John Howard Yoder (1927–1997)[13] are the texts I will analyze in this book as three paradigmatic models of how the Constantinian shift has been interpreted.

When the church was embraced by (or embraced) Constantine it was forced to rethink the relationship between the church and the Roman Empire. This was programmatically carried out by Eusebius, and his praise of the Constantinian shift found expression in his *Vita Constantini*. Augustine of Hippo, around a century later, reacted against Eusebius's interpretation of the Constantinian shift. In the *De Civitate Dei* Augustine laid out a grand view of history, in which a different interpretation of the Constantinian shift came to expression. In the *Vita Constantini* and the *De Civitate Dei* two paradigmatically different ways of interpreting the Constantinian shift were expressed. Glenn F. Chesnut, an American classicist with a special interest in ancient and medieval historiography, has suggested that Eusebius's and Augustine's approach to history came to form the two patterns according to which all Western history was written up through the middle ages and into the modern period.[14] A quite assertive statement that possibly exaggerates just how exemplary they came to be. However, that the two interpretations of the Constantinian shift laid out by Eusebius and Augustine came to form paradigmatic interpretations of this specific question up to early modernity, I hold to be a valid claim.

---

12. I refer to *De Civitate Dei contra Paganos* as *De Civitate Dei*. I am following the guideline for abbreviation of Augustine's works as laid out by the journal *Augustinian Studies* at Villanova University. This abbreviation goes back to the Italian name *De ciuitate dei libri uiginti duo* and is also utilized by the *Augustinus-Lexicon*. See Mayer, *Augustinus-Lexicon*, xi.

13. Yoder published much of his work in form of shorter essays.

14. "Eusebius and Augustine between them dominated historiographical theory and method for the entire Middle Ages and well into the modern period. It is difficult to exaggerate their importance: for a large part of the Middle Ages, had it not been for them, there would probably have been no histories written at all. Historians either copied one or the other of the two, or tried to combine them, or attempted to develop new genres whose seminal ideas nevertheless came from one or the other. Eusebius, and Augustine's reaction to him, set the stage for the entire complex history of medieval and early modern western historiography which followed." See Chesnut, "Eusebius, Augustine, Orosius," 709.

Yet, the current context has called for a new interpretation of the Constantinian shift. The American Mennonite theologian John Howard Yoder has produced such a contemporary interpretation, which has gained influence especially in Anglo-Saxon theology.[15] Yoder's interpretation of the Constantinian shift deals with many of the same questions that Eusebius and Augustine dealt with, but is still, as we will see, presenting yet another way of interpreting the Constantinian shift. Relevant for this book is furthermore the fact that Yoder not only interprets the Constantinian shift as a historical event but at the same time analyzes Eusebius's and Augustine's interpretations of the Constantinian shift.[16]

Eusebius, Augustine and Yoder are all theologians, for whom the study of history and their theological work is not clearly distinguishable. To various degrees their historical account is the modus in which they express their theological convictions.[17] Such an approach to the study of history might not live up to the requirements of modern historians. This should not prompt us to discard these sources, though, as they are still very useful for a church historian. First, such "theological history-writing" can actually, despite its lack in historical accuracy, provide knowledge of the historical events. Through the way these authors utilize history to make their theological points, it is possible to tease out insights about historical events. If their biases are taken into account, such texts can thus function as sources for gaining knowledge of historical events. Second, such "theological

---

15. Mark T. Nation puts it this way: "During the last half of the twentieth century John Howard Yoder emerged as one of the most influential theologians and ethicists of his generation." See Nation, "John Howard Yoder: Mennonite, Evangelical, Catholic," 357. It needs to be taken into account that Mark Nation himself is a Mennonite theologian, but even a critic of Yoder, Peter Leithart, acknowledges his stature: "John Howard Yoder (1927–1997) was for many years the world's most prominent theological proponent of pacifism and was probably the most influential Mennonite theologian who ever lived." See Leithart, *Defending Constantine*, 11. However, when commending Yoder it is of the highest necessity not to hide how Yoder was guilty in far-reaching sexual abuse. Most importantly in respect for the victims, but also in order to keep Yoder accountable to his own theological concerns. How this process must begin by listening to the stories of the victims, I will return to in the coming chapter on Yoder.

16. Alexander Sider points out that, "Eusebius of Caesarea and Augustine of Hippo are only slightly less central figures in Yoder's account of the age of Constantine than is Constantine himself. Indeed, Eusebius and Augustine are the dominant theological touchstones in Yoder's narration of the fourth and fifth centuries." See Sider, *To See History Doxologically*, 113.

17. The work of N. F. S. Grundtvig can be pointed to as a Danish equivalent for an approach to history, where events of the past are theologically engaged and interpreted.

history-writing" will, through the way history is used and presented, reveal the theological points of view of the author. Despite the fact that the material might not provide the most reliable historical account, the manner in which the three theologians interpret or use a historical event yields insights into their theological position. Both approaches will be utilized in this book, but as this book focus on the historiography the latter approach will be the dominant one, as I will explain further in the section on the theoretical framework.

Many sources could have been chosen, so why exactly these? First, I hold their interpretations to be paradigmatic in regard to how the Constantinian shift came to be interpreted in the church. The convenient way to schematize them would be to oppose Eusebius's (positive) and Yoder's (negative) evaluation of the Constantinian shift and argue that Augustine is the corrective to both of them. It is not exactly that simple. But it is, nevertheless, a fact that between the three of them they do represent main stances regarding how the Constantinian shift has been interpreted through the history of the church. In addition to being paradigmatic interpretations, in the sense that they represent how the Constantinian shift came to be interpreted throughout the history of the church, I suspect them to be paradigmatic in another way. That is, I wonder whether a coherent Christian theology might not allow for many other interpretations of the Constantinian shift than these three. In that sense they are paradigmatic both in a contingent historical sense and possibly in a systematic theological sense.

Other material could have been chosen, but a number of reasons can be given as to why this material suffices for representing the outlines of the important ways in which the Constantinian shift has been interpreted through the history of the church.[18] First, the texts of Eusebius, Augustine and Yoder provide satisfactory material for both an analysis of the

18. Other representatives than Eusebius, Augustine and Yoder of these three main stances on how to interpret the Constantinian shift could have been engaged. As representatives of the ancient debate for example Hippolytus of Rome (170–235), strongly hostile to the union of church and empire, and Melito of Sardis (died around 180), strongly in favor of the union of church and empire, could also have been analyzed. But given that they both lived before Constantine, and that their writings only have survived in fragmentary form, they will not be dealt with in this book. Regarding later sources also the writings of for example an early Anabaptist theologian like Menno Simons (1496–1561) could have been chosen, but none made the question of how to interpret the Constantinian shift a center of their theology quite as elaborately as Yoder, as he is the one to have put this question on the theological map again in contemporary theology.

historiography of the Constantinian shift and for an investigation of the theological underpinning affecting the interpretation of the Constantinian shift.

Second, they are all three specifically writing on the question of the Constantinian shift, even sharing detailed subcategories, which makes them excellent conversation partners. We will come to see how three main areas of contention are to be found in all three interpretations of the Constantinian shift: (a) How is the (in)visible church to be in the world? (b) What approach is the church to take on war? (c) How is the eschatological perspective of the gospel interpreted? Throughout questions pertaining to these subcategories continually surface in the works of all three theologians. This makes it possible to bring them into conversation without forcing the material into preconceived schemes.

Third, Eusebius, Augustine and Yoder approach the interpretation of the Constantinian shift in a similar manner. Not only do they engage the same questions, but methodologically they engage them in a similar fashion. As described above they namely all perceive the study of history to be a deeply theological enterprise. This structural trait makes them eminent conversation partners as both the same themes and the same questions weave into each other in the three texts.

With that said, Eusebius, Augustine and Yoder wrote in distinctly different contexts, and their unique historical setting has influenced their differing interpretations of the Constantinian shift. Despite their likeness in how they approach these questions, it is important to keep that variance in mind, in order not to skim over their distinct differences. At the same time as it is important to keep their similarity in mind too, in order not to ignore the commonalities in their interpretations of the Constantinian shift. Like all historical investigations, the choice of material leaves also this book in tension between the investigation of the isolated historical event with no connection to wider history, and an engagement with history that discards the historical context and attempts to explain all of history from one principle.

Three theological accounts of history from different periods of time are to be compared. It is a challenge to make three such different theological voices engage in conversation. At least it requires a proper framework. This is what I will look into now.

1.3 Methodology

It has now been established what material will be examined in this book and the reasons behind why this material is selected have been clarified, but methodological questions remain. Eusebius, Augustine and Yoder were situated in very different contexts and have very different ecclesial backgrounds—can their interpretations of the Constantinian shift be brought into conversation at all? Are they not too removed in place and time to be engaged in meaningful comparison? A theologian sensitive to the history of the church would hardly hold such a view.

The church was possibly the first globalized institution in history. However, it had a concept of globalization different from the one that is dominant today—the church (at its best) understood the importance of both the global and the local perspective.[19] When it comes to the sources chosen for this book, I have striven to follow this principle. None of the sources are directly addressing each other and are approaching the question

---

19. The church historically understood globalization in a manner very different from how it is understood today, informed as it now is by the logic of the market and big corporations. The financial logic of hyper-capitalism envisions globalization as a fluid cosmopolitan way of being, without any attachment to a specific place. As Fredric Jameson has argued, the global capitalist system is supported by the myth of the individual abstract person without body or culture; factors which only posits limits for the urge of capitalism to grow and spread into all of life's spheres. See Jameson, *Postmodernism*, 260–78. As a counter-reaction to such rootless cosmopolitanism, we have seen the rise of a number of right-wing parties all over Europe, which insist on human beings belonging only at one certain place. They rule out communities not bound to a specific place, and deny the existence of overarching international communities. The church (at its best) has from the outset presented a distinctly different vision of globalization. The early church was from the beginning a globalized institution, which upheld an ideal of stretching across boundaries of culture, class and gender (Gal 3:28, Matt 28:19–20). But it was at the same time committed to the place and the specifics of the locations of the various congregations. Contrary to the logic of big corporations, the local did not only serve the bigger structure, but was an end in itself. The church did not move away when a specific location had been "depleted of resources" or better opportunities presented themselves elsewhere, as multinational corporations tend to do today. This vision might present an ideal and in reality the Christian Church has often fallen into either a nationalist or an overly universal mistake. But it is nevertheless a fact that in Christian theology is to be found a vision of the relationship between global and local, which avoids both the mistake of abstract cosmopolitanism and local chauvinism; for a further development of this idea, see Luke Bretherton's exposition of the concept of Christian Cosmopolitanism in his *Christianity and Contemporary Politics*, 126–74. Likewise, the material dealt with in this book will be investigated in its specificity, but it will not be ignored how it can shed light on universal theological questions.

of the Constantinian shift with very different agendas. But they are, in very specific contexts, dealing with questions unified by universal theological concerns. One of the tasks of the theologian is to identify how what lies far away in place and time can be immediately relevant for the here and now. And this leads us on to the theoretical framework.

This book is set within three theoretical frameworks. These frameworks pertain to questions of how to do theology, which historical questions to ask and how to set the timeframe for a historical study. That these questions are connected will be made evident later. First I will deal with them one by one.

The concrete problems with which the church has to deal are the source from which the most interesting theological questions emerge. Through the history of the church, the most creative theological work has been done when concrete problems of the church pressed theologians to think anew about foundational questions of Christianity.[20] In the same way as medicine and law, for example, are dealing with questions pertaining to what goes on in the court houses and the hospitals, the questions of theology springs from the lived life of the church. When that connection is severed, theology is left to drag on an anemic existence. Does that mean theology is but a servant of the church? Not exactly. The discipline of theology needs some distance from the church in order to see it clearly and get the bigger picture. Academic theology's contribution to the church consists surprisingly often exactly therein that it can criticize the church. And only from a sufficiently independent point of view is it possible to maintain such a critical view.[21]

My conception of theology's direct dependence on the church draws inspiration from the so-called Yale School (also referred to by the broader term "postliberal theology") founded by Hans Frei and George Lindbeck, and their critique of the paradigm of secular modernity, or, more precisely, how theology reacted to modernity by compromising its tradition in return

---

20. Augustine's *De Civitate Dei*, Martin Luther's *Römervorlesung*, and the Confessing Church's *Barmer Bekenntnis* are but a few examples.

21. When following the approach to theology laid out here one has to keep an eye out for the pitfall, which Marc Bloch described this way: "Unfortunately the habit of passing judgments leads to a loss of taste for explanations." See Bloch, *Historian's Craft*, 140. Bloch was the historian who, with Lucien Febvre, founded the so-called Annales School of historical method named after the journal *Annales d'histoire* économique et sociale established in 1929.

for academic acceptance.²² By an ecumenical engagement of the theological tradition prior to the Enlightenment postliberal theology eludes the tiring schism in Anglo-Saxon theology between liberal and conservative approaches to theology, which emerged as a reaction to modern critical scholarship. Postliberal theology maintains furthermore that only when superseding this dichotomy, theology will have unique contributions to make to the wider academy.

One quality of postliberal theology is its attempt to break down the divides between the theological disciplines of biblical exegesis, church history and systematic theology and reinstate a unified theological approach held together by the task of providing answers to the multifaceted questions springing from the life of the church.²³ This book falls within the discipline of church history; but will not operate with a narrow separation of church history and systematic theology. In that respect this book is in line with how postliberal theology envisions the craft of theology. That leads on to the second point.

Certain theological underpinnings influenced how Eusebius, Augustine and Yoder interpreted a historical event like the Constantinian shift. Theological presuppositions was not the only factor influencing their interpretations, though. The influence determining how they interpreted the Constantinian shift can be classified in two categories. One category we can label the influence from sociological, economic, political etc. factors. To identify how such factors influenced the development of church and theology has been one of the virtues of the discipline of church history as it has

---

22. Martinson, "Postliberal Theology," 1818. For a succinct account of postliberal theology, see Mattias Martinson's entry "Postliberal Theology" in *Encyclopedia of Sciences and Religions*. For the primary initiating works, see Lindbeck, *Nature of Doctrine*, and Frei, *Eclipse of Biblical Narrative*. Though still maintaining its focus on exploring the Christian narrative, rather than engaging in apologetics, postliberal theology has moved forward in different ways today and Yale Divinity School and Duke Divinity School have become main proponents for two dissimilar developments, which differs on the question of whether a unified Christian interpretation of reality can be attempted. In relation to this, Yale theologian Kathryn Tanner has argued that the restriction of theology to reflect only on the experience of the church does not do justice to how human beings gain knowledge about God and the world. For the Yale position, see for example Tanner, *Theories of Culture*; for the Duke position, see for example, Hauerwas, *In Good Company*.

23. Former professor at Yale University David Kelsey's dogmatic tome *Eccentric Existence* is one of the most systematic works inspired by postliberal theology to have appeared. Kelsey here characterizes the life of the church as "primary theology," and the academic reflection over and critique of it as "secondary theology." See Kelsey, *Eccentric Existence*, 17–45.

been construed for the past two centuries. A second category we can label the influence from the theological presuppositions of the three theologians. Though hardly possible to separate succinctly, the focus of this book is directed toward the second category of influence on their interpretation of the Constantinian shift.

By applying the method of a close thematic reading, I analyze three interpretations of the Constantinian shift, and conclude as to which theological underpinnings and preconceived models of the church reveal themselves in Eusebius's, Augustine's and Yoder's interpretations. Such a project entails a careful reading of the three interpretations of the Constantinian shift that still not ignores the historical details. As this book is written within the discipline of church history and not systematic theology, such identification of theological structures will be pointed out along the way during the analysis of interpretations of the Constantinian shift found in the texts, but only made explicit and compared by the end of the book. That I am attempting to follow a post-liberal approach does not mean ignoring the structure in theological work that disciplinary boundaries can also bring with them.

By concluding with teasing out the theological tenets expressed in the three interpretations of the Constantinian shift, I am not suggesting that the interpretations are only or mostly driven by influence from what I classified as the second category of influence, i.e., the theological underpinning. All sorts of political, sociological, economic influence, what I labeled category one, exerts their influence on the three interpretations too—Eusebius was on very good terms with Constantine, to point out the most obvious example. But the aim of this book is not (a) to identify to what extent political, social etc. pressures played a role for the interpretation of the Constantinian shift.[24] Neither is it (b) to investigate the interplay between how a specific interpretation of the Constantinian shift reversely formed the theological presuppositions of the authors. Instead, I will analyze texts and look into what theological views and argumentative structures are revealed in these three interpretations of the Constantinian shift.[25]

---

24. For a succinct account of how all kind of politic considerations influenced the life and theology of the early church, see the renowned scholar on the fourth century Hal Drake's *Constantine and the Bishops*. Drake pointedly states that "the councils of the early church may have been subject to the Spirit in their content, but as blasphemous as it may sound, in getting things done even the Spirit had to bow to the rules of politics." See Drake, *Constantine and the Bishops*, xvii.

25. Once more, such an approach finds inspiration in the Postliberal narrative

As will become increasingly clear throughout this book, the writing of history and theology is intertwined. Deeply seated theological structures have exerted influence on how the Constantinian shift was interpreted throughout church history. An insight into these theological underpinnings will help cast light on why the Constantinian shift was interpreted the way it was. One could ask where such a research question is located within the discipline of academic church history? That leads us to the third point.

A contemporary renewed interest in the *longue durée* ties in with the way historical questions are posed in this book.[26] After having been ignored by the historical guild, which had lost faith in the possibility of any overarching narratives, ideas from the *longue durée* are now reemerging, and grand studies of history are being published again.[27] David Armitage and David Christian both identify extreme specialization in the field as well as the influence from academic ideals in the natural sciences and lately the influence from postmodern theory as three causes for the often prevalent distrust of grand historical perspectives.[28] They also agree that new digital

---

theological approach. This methodology does not hold that historical questions of how theological texts came to be are irrelevant, but, instead of stopping with such questions, goes on to investigate what is actually the theological content of the texts of the church. For an introduction to this approach within the discipline of biblical exegesis, see Davis and Hays, *The Art of Reading Scripture*.

26. The term *longue durée* was first used by Fernand Braudel in a 1958 article in the *Annales*. See Braudel, "Histoire et Sciences sociales: La longue durée," 725–53. In this article Braudel lamented how historians who focused only on shorter timespans (fifty years at the most), would come to ignore deeper continuities often underlying processes of change. See Armitage and Guldi, "Return of the *Longue Durée*: An Anglo-American Perspective," 6. For a recent study of the history the Annales school, see Burguière, *Annales School*—a study referred to by Georg Iggers as "without question the best history of the Annales movement to date." See Iggers, review of *The Annales School: An Intellectual History*. Burguière focuses on how the early founders (Bloch and Febvre) shared an interest in the history of mentalities, which became less prominent among later *Annales* historians. See Burguière, *Annales School*, 4–5. This book is thereby not the first to depart from exclusively applying the *longue durée* perspective to study the influence of "hard" factors like geography or economic structures.

27. Armitage, "What's the Big Idea?," 496–97. "In recent years there has been a resurgence of large-scale narratives in world history, global history, trans-national history, macro-history, or whatever we choose to call it." See Christian, "Return of Universal History," 15.

28. As this book will reveal, the abandoning of overarching accounts of history is the exception within the way historical accounts have been given in far the most part of Western history. As we will see, neither Eusebius nor Augustine shrink back from large historical narratives. Yoder too operates with a grand historical narrative, though a contemporary scholar.

tools provide historians with ways to make academically rigorous large-scale studies that was previously impossible.²⁹

An analysis of three interpretations of the Constantinian shift, though separated by centuries, will hold this book together. It will not be a classical study in the *longue durée* tradition, as I will not here be focusing on overarching sociological or geographical structures. But my methodological approach does connect to central tenets in a reemerging interest in the *longue durée*. The following quotation elucidates how this is the case:

> In a moment of ever-growing inequality, amid crises of global governance, and under the impact of anthropogenic climate change, even a minimal understanding of the conditions shaping our lives demands a scaling-up of our inquiries. As the *longue durée* returns, in a new guise with new goals, it still demands a response to the most basic issues of historical methodology—of what problems we selected, how we choose the boundaries of our topic, and what tools we put to solving the question. The power of memory can return us directly to the forgotten powers of history as a discipline to persuade, to reimagine, and to inspire . . . the new historians of the *longue durée* should be inspired to use history to criticize the institutions around us and to return history to its mission as a critical social science. History can provide the basis for a rejection of anachronisms founded on deference to longevity alone. Thinking with history—but only with long swathes of that history—may help us to choose which institutions to bury as dead and which we might want to keep alive.³⁰

At least three traits described by Armitage and Guldi are guiding this book. First, this book focuses on "long swathes" of history, comparing three different interpretations of the Constantinian shift expressed in very different points of time. Instead of analyzing fifty years of historiography I will be analyzing 1,500 years of historiography.³¹ Second, while adherents of intel-

---

29. See Armitage, "What's the Big Idea?"; and Christian, "Return of Universal History."

30. Armitage and Guldi, "Return of the *Longue Durée*," 45–46. For a succinct summary of ideas expressed in this article, see Arbesman, "Return of History at Long Timescales."

31. To be more precise, I will analyze the interpretation of the Constantinian shift at three specific times over a 1,600-year history (the fourth, the fifth and the twentieth century). This approach will at the same time allow us to pay attention to both the grand narrative of history and the contextual uniqueness of history. Such an approach to historical study is partly inspired by Yoder, without this implying necessarily sharing his

lectual history traditionally were hostile to *longue durée*, this animosity is not necessarily the case among new proponents of this approach. Armitage points out that, though maybe not straight forward, there can be effected "a greatly overdue rapprochement between intellectual history and the *longue durée*."[32] The connection between intellectual history and the theological study of the interpretation of the same historical phenomena over time, I believe to be fruitful. This book is concerned with how the concept of the Constantinian shift has been interpreted differently and has meant different things in different contexts, and thereby ties in with a *longue durée* approach to intellectual history. Third, this book shares the concern from the quote above that a historical study, ought "to persuade, to reimagine, and to inspire" regarding how we think about current institutions of society. Few subjects honor this principle better than one pertaining to questions of how to conceive of the relationship between church and state.

What ties together the theological theory for this book (the first point) and the historical theory (the third point), is the way the historical question of this book is asked (the second point)—i.e., focusing this book not on the historical events surrounding the Constantinian shift, but rather on the interpretation of these events, makes it possible to align questions of historical and theological interest. An analysis of how the Constantinian shift has been interpreted by Eusebius, Augustine and Yoder allows for a project comparing the same concept in very different periods of time.

Before we can begin unfolding this, though, we need to look at the definition of two concepts central to this book. When analyzing the historiography of the Constantinian shift, one is engaging two terms which can both be variously defined: "historiography" and "the Constantinian shift." Below I will provide a brief definition of how these terms are applied in this book.

The term historiography can carry two slightly different meanings, which can be distinguished as the narrow and the broad use. The narrow use is characterized by dealing with "the writing of history on writing history," i.e., the investigation of how history as a craft has been described and how the methods and theories of the craft have changed over time. The broad use of the term is characterized by dealing with the body of historical work on a specific topic (i.e., how historians have interpreted and narrated a certain period, phenomenon, etc.). A study of how historians have

---

interpretation of history. See Sider, *To See History Doxologically*, 128–29.

32. Armitage, "What's the Big Idea?," 497.

presented the story of the Roman Empire would serve as an example of the broad use of the term. Though closely related, these are two different perspectives. In this book I will utilize the term historiography in the second, broad sense. I will investigate work historical theologians have produced when accounting for the Constantinian shift. These two approaches cannot be separated, though, and the question of how Eusebius, Augustine and Yoder perceived the craft of history differently will likewise be dealt with in the analysis of their interpretations of the Constantinian shift.

The terms most central to a field of study are sometimes the ones hardest to define.[33] This principle also pertains to the study of the Constantinian shift. A question can be raised as to when the Constantinian shift took place. Was it with the *Edict of Milan* in 313, when Constantine legalized Christianity alongside other religions? Was it in 380, when Theodosius I made Christianity the official religion of the Roman Empire? Or was it in 392 when Theodosius I passed legislation that made all pagan worship illegal? In addition to such legal definitions, the Constantinian shift is also applied to denote a shift in the relationship between church and the secular state.[34] But exactly what that shift consists in is not clear either. Does the Constantinian shift mean *caesaropapism*; when a secular ruler is in control of the church?[35] Or is the opposite the case—that the Constantinian shift means *hierocracy*; when a secular ruler acquires legitimacy only when authorized by the church?[36] How the Constantinian shift is defined comes to the core of how it is interpreted.[37] Therefore it would not be appropriate to

33. The academic study of religion is a good example. There is in the field of Religious Studies no agreement as of how to define the term "religion." Yet, this does not hinder the field from developing and producing studies on religion. This goes to show how a term does not need a narrow definition in order to be used fruitfully.

34. To use the vocabulary of a "secular state" is an anachronism when writing about fourth-century material, since the dividing line between ecclesiastical and secular politico-military realms was not clearly defined by this point. See Chesnut, "Eusebius, Augustine, Orosius," 689. However, the term "secular" is employed in this book, as it functions as a readily understandable marker when differentiating between the church and the political realm. Such use of the word goes back to its Latin root *saeculum*; meaning "mundane" and "temporal." In part 3 I will revisit the debate on how to conceive of the *saeculum*.

35. Max Weber defines *Caesaropapism* as a secular ruler having total power over the church. See Swedberg, *Max Weber Dictionary*, 22.

36. Max Weber defines *Hierocracy* as a ruler legitimated by priests or as a high priest who is also king. See Swedberg, *Max Weber Dictionary*, 112.

37. In his dissertation on Yoder, history and ecclesiology, Alexander Sider made that poignantly clear with a question: "Why call Constantinianism a shift? Why not a

operate with a rigorously defined term, as this would distort the picture when analyzing different interpretations of the Constantinian shift. Instead of a narrow conceptual definition, a broad practical definition of the Constantinian shift is applied in this book. The Constantinian shift will thus be understood as referring to the political events and theological changes taking place during Constantine's ascendency in the late third and early fourth century.

One qualification needs to be made. Yoder uses the term Constantinian shift and Constantinianism also to denote a general shift in mentality, which continues to have ramifications throughout the history of the church until the present day.[38] For Yoder, the Constantinian shift thereby becomes both a historical and a theological term. Yet, also for Eusebius and Augustine the Constantinian shift, to a varying degree, becomes simultaneously a historical and a theological term, and the question of the relationship between a historical account and a theological account lies at the heart of this book. I will now provide a short outline of the book, and then commence the investigation of the historiography of the Constantinian shift and its theological underpinnings.

1.4 Structure

As mentioned already, Eusebius, Augustine and Yoder in their interpretations of the Constantinian shift deal with the same categories of questions. In order to make this similarity fruitful for the analysis, I will approach the three authors in a parallel manner. I will compare the texts in a five-fold structure, which will make both similarities and dissimilarities stand out. Parts 2–4 of the book follow such a five-fold structure: (a) An introduction to the theologian and his context will be found in the start of each part. (b) It will be succeeded by an analysis of that theologian's interpretation of the Constantinian shift, along the lines of similar subcategories. In order not to lose the reader in the thematic treatment of the work, a short outline will in each case be given in the beginning. (c) Then a preliminary conclusion on the analysis of the text can be made. (d) After such a close reading, an engagement with contemporary scholarly research will follow. Though contemporary research will be continually drawn in to aid the analysis, this

---

development? An evolution? A maturation? Each description is loaded, and each deploys a different narrative about the past." See Sider, *To See History Doxologically*, 107.

38. LeMasters, *Import of Eschatology*, 101.

will be a specific engagement with contemporary debates useful for this book. (e) At the end of each chapter a comparison to the previously analyzed interpretations of the Constantinian shift will be conducted.

Texts have their own will and can only be forced into such grids to a certain extent. This condition is also true here, and these five main sections do not entirely resemble each other throughout. Part 2 on Eusebius will necessary fall short on a fifth section, as there is no earlier analysis to compare it to. Part 3 on Augustine cannot be organized into exactly the same subcategories in the second section, due to the fact that Augustine's treatment of the Constantinian shift is structured a little different from Eusebius's and Yoder's.

The book thus follows a structure of rising complexity. Part 2 establishes the historical basics of the Constantinian shift and provides a close reading of the *Vita Constantini* in order to establish foundational material on the Constantinian shift. Part 3 provides an account of Augustine's critique of Eusebius's interpretations and compares the two interpretations. But only in part 4 will it be possible to conduct a proper comparison of the three interpretations and their theological underpinnings, all of which come together in the conclusion in part 4. This will lead up to part 5 of this book, which teases out overarching historical and theological points central for how the Constantinian shift is interpreted, and thereby connects to part 1 and the question of how to be "in the world but not of the world" from an ecclesiological perspective.

PART II

An Early Interpretation

2

Eusebius of Caesarea

2.1 Introduction

One of the first theologians who had to think through and frame questions anew regarding the relationship between church and the empire was Eusebius of Caesarea (ca. 260–339). Being a bishop around the time Constantine came into power made it necessary for him to reconsider a number of theological questions. Eusebius's interpretation of the relationship between the church and the Roman Empire is determined by a theology, and it is this theology in relation to the Constantinian shift I will examine. In order to accomplish this, I will look into how Eusebius in the *Vita Constantini* portrays Constantine and his acts as emperor and Christian, and examine what theological underpinning is expressed in this portrayal.

I have two theses to argue in this part 2 of the book. First, I intend to show how Eusebius was not just a sycophant, who gave up having a theological vision for his work, in order to please the emperor. Rather, Eusebius was a creative theologian who had a theological vision for his understanding of the relationship between the church and Roman Empire; a vision which was expressed in his interpretation of the Constantinian shift.[1] Second, I intend to demonstrate how Eusebius's theology was characterized

---

1. Such a reading of Eusebius is guided by a new approach within contemporary scholarship, according to which Eusebius is not just used as a source for historical questions or biographical questions pertaining to Constantine. First having engaged Eusebius's text will provide a foundation for looking into this shift in scholarship on Eusebius in section 2.5.

by perceiving the interests of the church and the Roman Empire as closely aligned.

To accomplish this, a few prefatory steps are necessary. Averil Cameron comments that "the early-fourth-century *Life of Constantine* by Eusebius, [is] a work overcriticized on historical grounds, and understudied as a literary text."[2] Though that might well be true, it is still necessary to commence what is to be a literary reading by first looking at some of the historical circumstances under which Constantine rose to power. After this a short outline of the *Vita Constantini* will move me closer to the text itself. Then I will be properly equipped to go into a close thematic reading of the *Vita Constantini*. After that is accomplished I will look into how this reading resembles a new evaluation of Eusebius's work in contemporary scholarship. At the end of the chapter a conclusion as to how Eusebius interpreted the Constantinian shift historically can be reached, and I can identify which theological underpinnings informed his interpretation.

Hal Drake points out that "while there were significant areas of agreement, the two men [Constantine and Eusebius] did not think identically on all issues, although thanks to the way Eusebius constructed the *Vita Constantini*, it is easy to conclude that they did, that Eusebius was simply a channel for Constantine's thinking."[3] Now we will begin by looking separately at Constantine and Eusebius, which will help spell out their differences.

2.2 Constantine

2.2.1 Constantine and His Time

When investigating how Eusebius interpreted and conceptualized the Constantinian shift it is important to remember that the Constantine depicted in the *Vita Constantini* is not the historical Constantine. Eusebius is emphasizing certain aspects of Constantine's history and personality that fits his theological project. To properly grasp how Eusebius interprets the Constantinian shift in the *Vita Constantini*, some basic knowledge of Constantine and his time is helpful. I will first give a short account of Constantine's personal history and the political circumstances under which he

---

2. Cameron, *Christianity and the Rhetoric of Empire*, 53.
3. Drake, *Constantine and the Bishops*, 383.

rose to power in the Roman Empire, and then briefly look at the number of Christians at the time of Constantine.

2.2.2 Constantine the Emperor

Constantine (ca. 272–337) was born in Naissus (present day Niš in the south east part of Serbia) as the son of Flavius Constantius, an officer in the Roman army, and Helena, a woman from a humble background. Both of Constantine's parents came to influence him in important ways: His father in helping him achieve the power as emperor and his mother in pointing him toward Christianity. In 293, Constantine's father entered the imperial college as a Caesar, which was a title just beneath that of Augustus. Thereby Constantius became part of the first so-called Tetrarchy created by Diocletian in 293, and Constantine came to reside at Diocletian's court.[4] The system was designed with two junior members, the Caesars, and two senior members, the Augusti, though the Caesars possessed most of the privileges of their senior colleagues.[5] The Tetrarchy was good in that it allowed for the sharing of ruling power, but the fault of the system was that it did not work properly, when an emperor came along, who did not want to share the power and had the means to realize such a desire.

In 306, Constantius died and Constantine stated his father had made him the new Augustus. Galerius, the Augustus over the eastern part of the empire, did not assent to this; and immediately demanded that Constantine should only be Caesar. This Constantine accepted, and patiently waited until stirs in the empire's power balance would put him in a position, where he could further advance.[6] This happened in 312, when Maxentius, who was the son of former Augustus Maximian, lost the battle at the Milvian Bridge and thereby lost Rome to Constantine, who had laid siege to the city.[7]

In 313, Constantine and his fellow Augustus, Licinius, are said to have promulgated the *Edict of Milan*. Thereby a change took place in the attitude toward Christianity in the Roman Empire and Constantine now gave freely from the imperial treasury to enlarge and to decorate churches.[8] He furthermore forbade gladiatorial shows and generally tried to appease the

---

4. Barnes, *Constantine and Eusebius*, 4.
5. Barnes, *Constantine and Eusebius*, 8.
6. Barnes, *Constantine and Eusebius*, 29.
7. Barnes, *Constantine and Eusebius*, 40–45.
8. Barnes, *Constantine and Eusebius*, 49.

Christians, which also included summoning the first council of Nicaea in 325.⁹

Constantine not only sought out the friendship of the church but also strove to achieve power of all of the Roman Empire. He therefore waged wars against his fellow Augustus, Licinius, who was the ruler of the eastern part of the empire. In 324 Constantine defeated Licinius and was thereby the sole ruler; a position he managed to hold until his death. During these relatively peaceful years, Constantine strove to build up his new capital, Constantinople (officially declared capital in 330) and, on request of his mother, to restore ancient holy places in Palestine, before he died in 337.

2.2.3 Constantine and the Church

Much ink has been spilled on the question of Constantine's possible conversion, despite the fact that posing this question does not do much to further the understanding of the Roman Empire during Constantine's reign. Whether Constantine personally identified as a Christian is not a question I will deal with here, as Constantine's personal faith, or lack thereof, is not that important in understanding the bigger background on which the *Vita Constantini* was written.¹⁰ What is more important for understanding the context of the *Vita Constantini* is to look into the development of the church among the population of the Roman Empire in the fourth century.

Constantine ruled an empire in which Christianity was becoming prevalent. In his book *The Rise of Christianity*, sociologist of religion Rodney Stark poignantly states that "rather than cause the triumph of Christianity, the emperor Constantine's 'Edict of Milan' was an astute response to rapid Christian growth that had already made them a major political force."¹¹ Various numbers have been suggested regarding the spread of Christianity during the fourth century. Stark suggests that by the mid-fourth century around half of the ca. sixty million Roman population were Christians.¹²

---

9. Barnes, *Constantine and Eusebius*, 53. Barnes depiction of Constantine as hospitable toward "the Christians" needs to be supplemented here. It is a fact that it was only a certain part of the church, which was favored by Constantine. Dissenting groups still suffered persecution, as was for example the case with the Arians later on. Barnes is of course aware of this fact, but in order to maintain a nuanced picture of the early church it needs to be pointed out.

10. In part 3, I will return to how earlier scholarship dealt with this question.

11. Stark, *Rise of Christianity*, 2.

12. Stark, *Rise of Christianity*, 10.

The classicist scholar on Eusebius Timothy Barnes points out that earlier scholarship suggested much lower numbers (Harnack is an example), but in contemporary scholarship these numbers have been revised upward.[13]

We can point out the historical facts when it comes to Constantine's political career and the statistics regarding the number of Christians. To be aware of these is helpful, but when reading the *Vita Constantini*, we are in the hands of Eusebius and there is no sure way of knowing whether Constantine appreciated or agreed with Eusebius.[14] Hopefully, though, the historical outline given above can provide a framework for understanding Eusebius's interpretation of the Constantinian shift as it comes to expression in the *Vita Constantini* in a blend of a historical account and a theological program.

2.3 Eusebius

2.3.1 Eusebius as Historian and Theologian

"Eusebius of Caesarea was the most important historical thinker in the Christian world prior to Augustine."[15] This is a pithy statement and its three elements can provide the structure for the following account of Eusebius. That Eusebius was from Caesarea will be the first point of entry as I look into his historical background. The fact that Eusebius was a historical thinker will serve as the second lead and I will look into how he understood the writing of history. That he was prior to Augustine, who was the theologian who later came to think about the question of the relationship between the church and the worldly empires in distinctly theological terms, will lead me to round off this section by looking into which genre the *Vita Constantini* falls.

2.3.2 Eusebius as a Theological Historian

Eusebius (ca. 260–339) became the bishop of Caesarea in Palestine in 314. It was an important city for both the church (Acts 10 tells the story of how the apostle Peter travels to Caesarea and Cornelius the Centurion becomes

---

13. Barnes, *Constantine and Eusebius*, 313–14; for an overview of this debate, see Stark, *Rise of Christianity*, 3–13.

14. O'Daly, *Augustine's City of God*, 9.

15. Chesnut, "Eusebius, Augustine, Orosius," 70.

a Christian) and for the Roman Empire (the city had already by the third century possibly as many as one hundred thousand inhabitants).[16] Caesarea was a city, which was safe from persecutions through most of Eusebius's life. This offered Eusebius the time to compose theological works in both biblical exegesis and church history. The most important of these being the *Historia Ecclesiastica*. When Eusebius died in 339 he was in the process of finishing the *Vita Constantini*. The work was begun only after Constantine died in 337, probably on request of Constantine's sons, and it was most likely Eusebius's successor as bishop, Acasius, who tidied the manuscript, put on the chapter headings and published the text.[17]

Eusebius was both in his exegetical work and in his historical work influenced by the theology of Origen and he inherited Origen's library.[18] Though, the relationship between Origen and Eusebius is not that simple to work out. Eusebius was a biblical scholar both by instinct and by training and was not by nature a philosopher like Origen.[19] But Eusebius was at various times accused for holding Arian or Semi-Arian beliefs, which might partially be traced back to his influence from Origen and his Logos-theology.[20]

In the *Vita Constantini*, Eusebius claims that he had a close relationship to Constantine and often was at his court. Contemporary scholarship has met Eusebius's claim of being close to the emperor with suspicion and pointed out that Eusebius met with the emperor only on four occasions,

---

16. Barnes, *Constantine and Eusebius*, 82.

17. Barnes, *Constantine and Eusebius*, 265. In this book, I cite the English translation of the *Vita Constantini* by Averil Cameron and Stuart G. Hall published in 1999. It is based on Friedhelm Winkelmann's critical edition of the *Vita Constantini* originally from 1975 and revised in 1991; Winkelmann's edition supersedes the earlier critical edition by Ivar August Heikel from 1902. The textual transmission of the *Vita Constantini* relies predominantly on four manuscripts and references to the *Vita Constantini* in later texts by later historians; especially by the fifth-century historian Socrates of Constantinople. Section II:24–II:42 of *Vita Constantini* is an exception, as it has survived in multiple copies. A succinct account of the textual history of the *Vita Constantini* can be found in Cameron's *Life of Constantine*, 50–53; and an elaborate grapical illustration of the history of the textual transmission can be found in Winkelmann's *Eusebius Werke*; see Eusebius, *Eusebius Werke*, XXV.

18. Cameron and Hall, *Introduction and Commentaries to "Life of Constantine,"* 2.

19. Barnes, *Constantine and Eusebius*, 94.

20. Eusebius had come to the Council in Nicaea under the provisional sanction of excommunication due to his Arian leanings. Constantine took the position that Eusebius, and two other bishops put under the same provisional ban, should be allowed into the council, which in fact did happen. See Barnes, *Constantine and Eusebius*, 216.

though the question of the exact relationship between Constantine and Eusebius is still a contended one.[21] Whether or not the historical facts of Eusebius's account is true is not the main question in this book; and yet, to be aware of where Eusebius is located historically provides a better background for understanding his presentation of the Constantinian shift in the *Vita Constantini*. This leads us to questions regarding the genre of the *Vita Constantini*, which is the last question to be treated before moving into the analysis of the text.

2.3.3 The Genre of the Vita Constantini

Eusebius was no bad rhetorician and he was clearly influenced by contemporary rhetorical models of how to compose a panegyric.[22] The *Vita Constantini* constitutes a combination of multiple classical genres. It is at the same time a *bios* (the ancient genre of biography), and an *encomium* (an appraisal of a ruler), and a historical account.[23] The *Vita Constantini* falls between these three genres. Though similar to many contemporary pieces of literature, this mixing of the genres makes the *Vita Constantini* a rather unique work. The *Vita Constantini* not only shares traits from the classical genres, but also combines Roman classical writing of the panegyric with the Christian hagiography.[24]

Both panegyric and hagiography can be used to describe the literary move Eusebius makes when he draws a parallel between Constantine and Moses, on which the *Vita Constantini* is relying at multiple instances.[25] For example: Eusebius recounts how Moses was born in a hostile country,

---

21. Barnes, *Constantine and Eusebius*, 266. Hal Drake cites Brian Warmington for pointing out that four is actually a rather high number of documented meetings between Eusebius and Constantine, given the limited knowledge passed down on such topics. In regard to Ossius of Cordoba, the appointed "adviser" of Constantine in theological affairs, even fewer meetings with Constantine can be documented. Drake points to this to make clear that when Eusebius sometimes glosses over or gets fact wrong it might not be due to lack of knowledge but rather due to deliberate choices grounded in his theological project. See Drake, *Constantine and the Bishops*, 370–71.

22. For a thorough account of the various influences on Eusebius's rhetorical style, see Penner, "Rhetoric of God in History," 16–33.

23. Cameron and Hall, *Introduction and Commentaries*, 30.

24. Cameron and Hall, *Introduction and Commentaries*, 31.

25. Averil Cameron points out that the interconnection between hagiography and panegyric is more subtle than often observed. See Cameron, "Eusebius' *Vita Constantini*," 151.

but was raised by God to lead his people home. He depicts Constantine's fate as similar to this. Constantine was raised up by God to lead the Christians into a new time and a new land.[26] Likewise Eusebius compares the drowning of Maxentius, Constantine's opponent, to the Red Sea closing over Pharaoh's Army in Exodus 15:5.[27] These panegyric and hagiographic traits of the *Vita Constantini* consolidate the image of Constantine as a ruler, whose interests are aligned with God's interests. Another famous example of Eusebius's appraisal of Constantine brilliantly shows how he combines sun worship and christological imagery into a panegyric description: "Just as the sun rises and spreads the beams of its light over all, so also Constantine shone forth with the rising sun from the imperial palace, as though ascending with the heavenly luminary, and shed upon all who came before his face the sunbeams of his own generous goodness."[28] This quotation beautifully carries us into our reading of the *Vita Constantini*.

2.4 Eusebius's Interpretation of the Constantinian Shift

In the thematic reading of the *Vita Constantini* I want to focus on the themes of church and empire, the emperor and God, and theology and politics. Before engaging these overarching themes, a short outline of the book will prove useful. The *Vita Constantini* does not follow a straight narrative pattern. As a reader one rather gets the feeling of reading a narrative often being interrupted by various excurses and anecdotes. That is no wonder, since this structure resembles the way the text came into existence, as Eusebius at various times returned to his work and added and revised material.[29] This compositional trait can make the idea of an outline of the text seem a preposterous task, but the outline will be guided by Eusebius's interpretation of the Constantinian shift, as this focus will serve to give the outline a structural center.

---

26. *VC* I:12; when citing the *Vita Constantini*, I refer to book, chapter, sub-chapter; for example "book 4, chapter 3, sub-chapter 2": *VC* IV:3.2. These divisions date back to the earliest versions of the text, though the classifications of the chapters differ slightly. I follow Winkelmann's classification.

27. *VC* I:38.

28. *VC* I:43.3.

29. Giorgio Pasquali already in 1910 proved how the *Vita Constantini* was not written as one coherent work, but this insight was chiefly ignored until Winkelmann pointed it out again in 1962. See Barnes, *Constantine and Eusebius*, 96–98.

VC I:1–I:19 provides an introduction to Constantine. It is from the beginning pointed out how pious Constantine was. In these opening paragraphs, the theme of the work is introduced: How Constantine at the same time is a good leader and a pious man. Eusebius compares Constantine to Moses, who, in the same way as Constantine grew up at Diocletian's court, was at Pharaoh's court and came to be a righteous leader. Eusebius then gives an account of Constantine's father, Constantius's good reign, and points out how Constantius did not partake in the suppression of the church. *VC* I:20–I:41 provides first an account of how Constantine joined his father's court and then a much-abbreviated account of how he rose to become Caesar. The narrative moves on to describe how Constantine waged war against Maxentius. Before the battle of the Milvian Bridge outside of Rome, God reveals himself to Constantine. Constantine wins the battle and enters Rome and the Arch of Constantine is erected to commemorate the victory. *VC* I:42–48 gives a short account of how Constantine participated as an equal in the councils of the church and let people speak out against him. Constantine took care of the churches and God repaid him for his favor. *VC* I:49—II:18 accounts for Constantine's wars against his fellow Augustus, Licinius. It is recounted how Licinius was persecuting the Christians, and how God repels Licinius's attacks on Constantine. Eusebius recounts how some of Licinius's men came to believe in God. *VC* II:19–II:60 tells how the persecution of Christians ended when Constantine came to reign over the whole Roman Empire. A letter from Constantine to provincials in the eastern part of the empire, dictating that what has been taken from the Christians during persecution is to be given back, is inserted in the *Vita Constantini* in its entirety here. Thereafter follows another letter against polytheistic worship. *VC* II:61—III:23 deals predominantly with the Arian churches' teachings in North Africa and the convening of the council of Nicaea (325). This account is interrupted by an account of how Constantine is a ruler much better than Licinius. *VC* III:24–III:66 gives an account of how Constantine rediscovered the biblical locations in Palestine and built churches there. Furthermore, it provides an account of how Constantine suppressed the non-Christian groups. *VC* IV:1—IV:13 follows up on the description of Constantine's Christian virtues by recounting how he was a good emperor. His success as a ruler is illustrated by his fame and correspondence with the Persian king. *VC* IV:14-IV:39 tells how Constantine both had personal piety, but also generously extended his favor to the churches in the form of an advantageous legislation. *VC* IV:40–IV:52

finishes the story of Constantine's life by recounting how he was loved in all of the empire and how his sons were prepared for succession. IV:53–IV:73 gives an account of how Constantine is baptized shortly before his death and describes the elaborate funeral arrangements and his lying-in-state. *VC* IV:74–IV:75 ends the *Vita Constantini* by pointing out that a pious man and magnificent ruler like Constantine never existed before, and he achieved things no one ever had achieved before.[30]

2.4.1 Church and Empire

Does the Constantinian shift mean that the secular realm is influenced by and takes over the ethics of the church, or does it mean that the church accepts the praxis of the secular ruler? Is what happens at the Constantinian shift the church conforming to the empire or the empire conforming to the church? From the perspective of a Max Weber these two perspectives were antithetical, but for Eusebius, such a question might never arise at all. In Eusebius's presentation the interest of the Roman Empire and the interest of the church point in the same direction; they are in harmony. One might object and argue that surely cannot hold true for all the ventures of the empire. At least when it comes to one of the most fundamental practices of a secular empire: that of conquering new land, Eusebius would not conceive of the interests of the church and the Roman Empire as harmonious? But as we will see below it is precisely the way Eusebius describes Constantine's conquests of new land that serves to illustrate most profoundly how Eusebius interprets the Constantinian shift as an alignment of the interests of the empire and the church.

2.4.1.1 The State Taking Over the Church or the Church Taking Over the State?

At the beginning of his career, Constantine had conquered the western part of the Roman Empire—where the sun sets. Toward the end of his life he undertook a military campaign to conquer Persia—where the sun rises.[31] In this last campaign toward the goal of a universal empire, Eusebius recounts

---

30. For this short outline of the *Vita Constantini* I have found partial inspiration in Timothy Barnes's categorization of the chapters; see Barnes, "Panegyric, History and Hagiography." See also Barnes, *Constantine and Eusebius*, 95.

31. *VC* IV:50.

how Constantine called in the help of the bishops: "They [the bishops] said that they would only too gladly accompany him as he wished, and not shrink back, but would soldier with him and fight at his side with supplications to God."[32] In Eusebius's representation the bishops share the interests of the ruler, and they do not have a problem in assisting Constantine in the quest for new land.

But according to Eusebius it was not only the leadership of the church who were happy with Constantine's conquering, as also the common people in the eastern part of the empire, previously ruled by Licinius, were happy that Constantine gained dominance there. Eusebius writes:

> all those in our part saw before their eyes those things which they had previously heard were being done in the other half of the Roman Empire, and had called the beneficiaries happy, praying that they too might some time enjoy the same; and now they also could deem themselves blessed, confessing that a strange new thing, such as the whole history of the world on which the sun shines had never told before, had illuminated the mortal race in so great an Emperor. Such were their feelings.[33]

The general pattern of thought in this quotation reveals that for Eusebius the Constantinian shift was interpreted neither as the church taking over the state nor the state taking over the church, but rather as a population welcoming a development, meaning that the head of the state was now sharing their values.[34] According to Eusebius's account, the Constantinian shift simply was for the common good, as it was in the interest of both the church and the Roman Empire.

2.4.1.2 The Common Good

Discussions of what "the common good" consists of are prevalent within the discourse of what society is to look like. What the common good looks

---

32. *VC* IV:56.3. The word translated as "fight" goes back to the Greek word συνἀγωνίζομαι. The semantic range of this word stretches from "aid" or "succor to fight on the same side" or "join in the action." See συνἀγωνίζομαι in Liddell and Scott, *Greek-English Lexicon*.

33. *VC* II:22.

34. If the numbers examined in the previous section regarding the spread of early Christianity holds true, there was in fact some historical basis to Eusebius's portrayal of Constantine as in agreement with the inhabitants of the land he conquered.

like is the question that fruitful political debate turns around. It is a question that might be rephrased as "how do we most beneficially organize our common life together"? Now, to what extent is the church to be engaged in this debate? On one hand it can be argued that the church is part of society and therefore has to chime in and take responsibility for and influence the direction in which society is moving. On the other hand, though, it can also be argued that the church is a pilgrim on this earth, and its ethics and its interpretation of this world is therefore so different that the church ought not attempt to control or direct where society is going, since doing so will compromise the commission of the church. How one views the obligations of the church to pursue the common good for society is indicative for how one interprets the Constantinian shift. Eusebius belongs to the first category, as he believes that the church can and ought to gain influence over the direction in which society moves.

Eusebius points out how Constantine's victory over Maxentius in Rome leads to that "all the nations" were set free from the evils who formerly oppressed them and "with one single voice they all acknowledged the common good [κοινός ἀγαθός] of mankind which by God's grace had dawned in Constantine."[35] In Eusebius's interpretation the common good of mankind has been expressed in Constantine; the ruler of the Empire. In this quotation we see that for Eusebius the difference between what is the common good and what is the good of the empire coincide. Furthermore, Eusebius describes how "the Emperor judged that the prayers of the godly made a great contribution to his aim of protecting the general good, so he made the necessary provision of these, becoming himself a suppliant for God."[36] For Eusebius the prayers from "the godly" are in congruence with the aim of the emperor and can be a great contribution toward the aim of protecting the general good.

For Eusebius the common good is expressed in Constantine and served by the prayers of the Christians. Such a unison view of the interests of the church and the Roman Empire Eusebius can only hold as long as the interests of the church and the state are pointing in the same direction. In

---

35. *VC* I:41.2. Eusebius was acquainted with the writings of Aristotle, and it is plausible that Eusebius, in his account of the common good, is inspired by Aristotle, especially Aristotle's *Nicomachean Ethics*. See Chesnut, "Eusebius, Augustine, Orosius," 706. For an account of how the concept of the common good later became an integral part of theological ethics and political theory, see Hollenbach, *Common Good*, 3–31.

36. *VC* IV:14.2.

some contexts they might do so, but, as we will see in part 3 of this book, it might not always be that straight forward.

2.4.2 Church and Emperor

2.4.2.1 THE RELATIONSHIP BETWEEN THE CHURCH AND THE EMPEROR

The Council at Nicaea (in 325) can serve as an example of a situation, in which both the secular ruler and the church had a common interest. It was necessary to establish a concord in the church in order to quiet down the doctrinal disagreements, which led to much disturbance that was problematic both for the church internally and for the peace of the empire. Eusebius had his own agenda, when it came to the depiction of how Constantine participated in the proceedings of the council at Nicaea. Eusebius states that at the council Constantine "took his seat among them [i.e., the delegates] as if he were one voice among many, dismissing his praetorians and soldiers and bodyguards of every kind, clad only in the fear of God and surrounded by the most loyal of his faithful companions."[37] Eusebius admits that Constantine did summon the bishops for the Council in Nicaea; and yet he is quick to add that Constantine did not use his power as emperor to push through any decisions. According to Eusebius's depiction, Constantine took care only of what can be termed "the external affairs of the church" (organizational structure), but did not meddle in what can be termed "the internal affairs of the church" (theology). In Eusebius's interpretation of the Constantinian shift, the emperor becomes a facilitator helping the church to organize itself and manage its affairs. Eusebius does not want to portray Constantine exerting any improper influence on the church. Making this distinction between inner and outer affairs of the church enables Eusebius to acknowledge Constantine's power without depicting him as taking over the church.[38]

37. *VC* I:44.2. See also *VC* III:12–13 for a further account of Constantine' participation in the council.

38. Such a distinction between the internal and the external affairs of the church can today still be found in countries with a state church; for example a country like Denmark. The underlying idea is that the state is in charge of "the outer affairs" and the bishops are in charge of "the inner affairs." It is interesting to note how a close relationship between church and state from the very beginning apparently called for such a distinction between inner and outer affairs of the church. A distinction that throughout history often has proved difficult to draw. To say the least.

Another example of the way Eusebius depicts Constantine's involvement in church politics can be found in the fact that he chose to include in the *Vita Constantini* a letter that Constantine sent to Arius (ca. 256–336) and Alexander of Alexandria (patriarch of Alexandria from 313 to his death around 328).[39] In the letter, Constantine chides Alexander and Arius for the divisions they are causing; due to endless discussions over theological issues that are "extremely trivial and quite unworthy of so much controversy."[40] Constantine clarifies that he is not trying to force them to come to agreement "on every aspect of this very silly [λίαν εὐήθης] question, whatever it actually is."[41] Instead Constantine urges them to find mutual ground, and, like the philosophers, realize that they do agree on basic principles.[42] Eusebius thus describes Constantine as one calling for peaceful coexistence in the church, instead of theological strife where there is no need for it. Constantine is thus depicted as a ruler who wants peaceful coexistence in both the church and the empire.[43]

Eusebius's depiction of Constantine's attitude at the council and his choice to include the letter to Arius and Alexander in the *Vita Constantini* provide clues as to how Eusebius interprets the Constantinian shift. Within scholarship up to the early 1980s, it was common to interpret Eusebius's attitude as overly servile toward the empire and subservient to the secular ruler. Contemporary scholarship on Eusebius, however, has moved "beyond the trite assessments of Eusebius as court theologian and sappy

---

39. As a historical note it can be pointed out how Eusebius states that the letter is addressed to Alexander and Arius personally, but the possibility exists that it was actually written to the Council at Antioch in the spring of 325. See Cameron and Hall, *Introduction and Commentaries*, 250. Scholarly literature earlier viewed the documents included in the *Vita Constantini* as inauthentic, but they are now by most scholars accepted as genuine. See Cameron and Hall, *Introduction and Commentaries*, 18.

40. *VC* II:68.2.

41. *VC* II:71.6. According to *A Greek-English Lexicon* the adjective εὐήθης also carries the meanings "absurd" and "foolish." See Liddell and Scott, *Greek-English Lexicon*.

42. *VC* II.71.2. That Eusebius might not have found these theological issues as trivial as Constantine can be learned by paying attention to the detail that Eusebius is not using his own words to argue that these theological questions were silly. Instead Eusebius is using the rhetorical trick of inserting a letter from Constantine to express this view. It can be supposed that this was a delicate matter for Eusebius, due both to his Arian leanings, but also, as pointed out earlier, due to the fact that Eusebius himself was a theological thinker.

43. It is telling that Eusebius himself does not manage to keep separate Constantine's interference in "the external" and "the internal" matters of the church. In order to keep peace in the church, Constantine had also to engage "the internal" matters of the church.

sycophant of the first Christian emperor."[44] This development is in line with what we saw above: Eusebius wants to portray the emperor as straightening up and helping out the church, since the interest of both the church and the state is to avoid strife and find peaceful coexistence, but this does not imply that Eusebius is pandering to Constantine. In Eusebius's interpretation, the interest of the Roman Empire and the interest of the church simply align. Such congruent interests between God and the Roman Empire naturally puts the emperor in a rather exceptional position.

2.4.2.2 THE SPECIAL RELATIONSHIP BETWEEN THE EMPEROR AND GOD

From the very outset of the *Vita Constantini* Constantine is depicted as standing in a special relationship with God. Constantine helps God and God helps Constantine: "Thus then the Emperor, serving God the overseer of all with his every action, took untiring care of his churches. God repaid him by putting all the barbarian nations beneath his feet."[45] Eusebius states that Constantine "alone among all those who have ruled the Roman Empire, became a friend [φίλος] of the all-sovereign God."[46] Eusebius portrays Constantine as the first emperor to enjoy this special relationship with God.

Eusebius furthermore often refers to Constantine as "the Godbeloved" (θεοφιλής).[47] In addition to Arian theology, Eusebius was influenced by Platonist philosophical ideas. In line with these ideas Eusebius understood Constantine as a worldly reflection of the heavenly ruler. Eusebius interpreted Constantine's monarchical rule over the entire civilized earth as the "icon" or image of God's sole monarchical rule over the universe.[48]

In Eusebius's other writings this imagery becomes even more pronounced. Throughout Eusebius's oration *De Laudibus Constantini* Constantine is often likened to Christ; Constantine's earthly empire replicates

---

44. Johnson and Schott, *Eusebius of Caesarea*, 12. We will look further into this important change in the scholarship on Eusebius later.

45. *VC* I:46.

46. *VC* I:3.4. The word φίλος furthermore carries the meaning of "a beloved one" or "an ally." Both these additional meanings of the Greek word substantiates Eusebius's depiction of a relationship of collaboration between God and Constantine. The reference calls to mind the figure of the *comes*; the companion which was an mandatory person for a successful emperor in the late empire; see Drake, *Constantine and the Bishops*, 379.

47. *VC* I:10.1.

48. Chesnut, "Eusebius, Augustine, Orosius," 702.

the heavenly kingdom insofar as the monotheism of the heavenly kingdom is reflected in the monarchical empire of Constantine.[49] Helena, the mother of Constantine, is also in the *Vita Constantini* described by Eusebius with the likeness of a mother of a God.[50] No matter whether Eusebius was influenced by Arianism or Platonist philosophy, the result was that Constantine came to be understood as standing in close relationship to the divine.[51] Again, Eusebius needs to be read properly. Eusebius compares Constantine to Christ, he does not say that Constantine is in fact God. A minor but important difference, as it proves Eusebius is still holding church and empire distinct, though they are closely aligned.

Toward the end of the *Vita Constantini* Eusebius describes how coins were minted, of which one depicted Constantine "like a charioteer on a quadriga, being taken up by a right hand stretched out from above."[52] Numismatic evidence bears witness to the historical accuracy of Eusebius's description of the coin, but more important for this book is the question of what Eusebius wanted to express by mentioning these coins?[53] The image on the coin draws on the concept of apotheosis: the custom of deification of

---

49. O'Daly, *Augustine's City of God*, 9. As we will see in the next part of the book, this way of conceiving the relationship between the heavenly kingdom and an earthly kingdom was something Augustine would later strongly turn against.

50. VC III:46.2–3. Helena came to play a great role in the later mythology surrounding Constantine. She came to be venerated for building Churches in Palestine (mentioned by Eusebius in VC III:25–42), by which she oriented the interest of the Christian world toward the geographical locations of the biblical narratives that had, up to that time, not received much attention. Furthermore, her reportedly inspired discovery of the true cross helped to emphasize the understanding of God as directly intervening in Constantine's reign. See Fowden, "Last Days of Constantine," 170.

51. In his famous book *Der Monotheismus als politisches Problem* Erik Peterson argued that it was because of the inspiration from non-trinitarian theology, that Eusebius was especially prone toward one ruler over both empire and church on earth, in the same way as there was one monarch in heaven. See Peterson, *Der Monotheismus als politisches Problem*, 81–100. Though an enticing analysis, Alfred Schindler has later pointed out that Peterson's study was influenced by an animosity toward a state-church connection, and fueled by the political situation in 1930s Germany. Eusebius did not associate his alignment of the empire and the church with his Arian views; for example his parallel between the Trinity and Constantine's rule (VC IV:2) strongly counters Peterson's claim. See Frend, review of *Monotheismus als politisches Problem?*, 252. To make a direct connection between Eusebius's Arian leanings and his interpretation of the Constantinian shift thus seems hasty.

52. VC IV:73.

53. For a depiction of the coin, see Cameron and Hall, *Introduction and Commentaries*, 346.

a deceased ruler.⁵⁴ Even though Constantine was not deceased at the time the coins were minted, the imagery still creatively applies this language of apotheosis to express a certain relationship between Constantine and God. On the coin this Roman imagery of deification blends with Christian imagery. The picture of the hand stretched out from above and the emperor moving toward it in his four horse chariot connects with Christian imagery of heavenly ascent.⁵⁵ Such a blend of images as found on the coin sums up too Eusebius's thinking about the Constantinian shift: God and Constantine are reaching out to each other. The plan of the Christian ruler and the plan of the Christian God are in unison and since they have common objectives, God and Constantine are working toward communal goals.

2.4.2.3 THE PERSONAL PIETY OF THE EMPEROR

To properly convey the image of a close relationship between God and Constantine Eusebius goes into great detail to describe Constantine's piety.⁵⁶ But the piety of Constantine also becomes constituent for how Eusebius interprets the Constantinian shift. For Eusebius, Constantine serves as a model in piety for all of the inhabitants of the nations: "By him [Constantine] he [God] cleansed humanity of the godless multitude, and set him up as a teacher of true devotion to himself for all nations, testifying with a loud voice for all to hear, that they should know who God is."⁵⁷ Eusebius in this way portrays Constantine's piety as a help toward both strengthening the empire and propagating the Christian faith.

At the council of Nicaea two major issues were dealt with besides the Arian question: the question of the Melitian schism and the deciding on a method to calculate the date for Easter. Eusebius describes how the Christian church had suffered a split regarding this question. This led to some Christians feasting during the time others were fasting.⁵⁸ That the church had not been able to agree on this question on its own, according to Eusebius was one of the reasons Constantine summoned the Council of Nicaea,

---

54. Cameron and Hall, *Introduction and Commentaries*, 349.

55. Both the hand from heaven and the image of ascend in chariot are standard imagery in Christian art. See MacCormack, *Art and Ceremony in Late Antiquity*, 124.

56. Averil Cameron is inclined to agree with Timothy Barnes that the *Vita Constantini* can be said to have "pioneered the idea of hagiography." See Cameron, "Eusebius' Vita Constantini," 169.

57. *VC* I:5.2.

58. *VC* III:18.6.

where the issue was finally settled. This made it easy for Eusebius to depict Constantine as a pious helper of the church.[59] Eusebius lauds Constantine and says that "alone of those on earth Constantine appeared as his [i.e., God's] agent for good."[60] Thus in addition to Constantine's piety benefiting the general population, Eusebius's depiction of Constantine's actions shows how his piety is interpreted to be simultaneously beneficial for the church. Constantine's piety does not lead to a questioning of suppressive power structures in society but is interpreted by Eusebius to be congruent with the interest of the empire.

A vast amount of further examples could be given as to how Eusebius depicts Constantine in a favorable manner. Instead, I will here point out an example of the opposite nature when it comes to the deeds of Constantine. Eusebius leaves out one of Constantine's more impious acts but he has a theological reason for doing so. When Constantine is victorious at the battle at the Milvian Bridge, his son Crispus played a substantial part in the battle.[61] Eusebius does not mention Crispus's contribution to the battle anywhere in the *Vita Constantini*. In fact he does not mention Crispus, or Crispus's mother Fausta, at all. This omission has to do with the fact that Constantine in all probability played a role in the death of both of them.[62] It is hazardous to draw *ex silentio* conclusions from historical texts, but here the absence is so striking that it seems safe to venture a suggestion.

Had Eusebius dared to include the story of a filicide committed by Constantine in the *Vita Constantini*, not only would it go against the genre convention of a panegyric but it could quite possibly have been dangerous for him too.[63] In a remark on the omission of any mention of Crispus and

---

59. Even though the delegates—Eusebius says more than 250 bishops were represented—"dashed like sprinters from the starting line, full of enthusiasm" to join the council (*VC* III:6.2), they apparently showed less fervor in implementing the council's decision of how to calculate the date of Easter, as it took several hundred years for the method of calculation from Nicaea to finally gain acceptance (the fact that the Orthodox Church still celebrates Easter at a different time than the Western church has instead to do with the Justinian Calendar, as agreement does exist to calculate the date of Easter based on the paschal full moon). For a thorough account of the discussion around when to celebrate Easter, see Cameron and Hall, *Introduction and Commentaries*, 259–61.

60. *VC* III:5.2.

61. Cameron and Hall, *Introduction and Commentaries*, 273–74.

62. Cameron and Hall, *Introduction and Commentaries*, 292–93.

63. Though, as both Constantine and Eusebius were dead before the final editing of the *Vita Constantini* was done, a threat to Eusebius's safety was not impending. See Eusebius, *Life of Constantine*, 9.

Fausta, historian of the Byzantine era Paul Stephenson expresses the traditional view on Eusebius. Stephenson states: "Eusebius, ever the sycophant, mentions neither Crispus nor Fausta in his *Life of Constantine*, and even wrote Crispus out of the final version of his *Ecclesiastical History*, where he had appeared in an earlier version [X.9.4]."[64] It is true that we can deduct from the omission that Eusebius did not want to portray Constantine in a negative way, and would therefore conceivably omit elements which did not fit the picture. But does it follow from this that Eusebius was a sycophant, who just wanted to please the emperor? Not necessarily. Eusebius had a theological vision for how the Constantinian shift was to be interpreted, and this vision would not encompass Constantine perpetrating an action that would come across as blatantly impious. Drake has argued that Eusebius generally was working within a "totalizing discourse," according to which all of history is interpreted by means of one explanation, and all voices that do not fit that explanation are silenced.[65] Such a totalizing discourse is at play in the *Vita Constantini* too. I believe this totalizing discourse in the *Vita Constantini* can be identified in a theological presupposition that states the interest of the Roman Empire and the interest of the church have come together in Constantine. Such a totalizing theological discourse does not allow Eusebius to mention a filicide committed by Constantine.

As pointed out above, Eusebius uses Moses as an exemplar for his description of Constantine, and yet even the biblical narratives depict Moses as blameworthy.[66] Eusebius's theological vision allows him to follow the genre conventions of the panegyric and describe Constantine favorably in a more one-sided way than even Moses, the founder of Judaism, is depicted in the Old Testament. This stylistic trait might here be taken as a hint that Eusebius's interpretation of the Constantinian shift is problematic in regard to how the realities of multiple interests coincide in history.

That said, we have now seen three examples of how Eusebius portrays Constantine's piety: as a helper of the church in organizing councils, not as

---

64. Stephenson, *Constantine*, 220. This makes the conclusion drawn on the silence of Eusebius a bit more solid, as it can be ruled out that his silence was due to unacquaintedness of the existence of Crispus and Fausta. For an account of the depiction of Crispus and Fausta in other contemporary sources, see Cameron and Hall, *Introduction and Commentaries*, 236.

65. Drake, *Constantine and the Bishops*, 360.

66. The fact that Moses is not allowed to enter the promised land has traditionally been interpreted as a punishment for a committed sin. What exactly that sin should be has been debated for millennia; see Anisfeld, "Why Was Moses Barred."

the instigator of the death of his son and wife, and as comparable to Moses. Apart from genre conventions, why is it so important to Eusebius to stress the piety of Constantine? The answer can be found in Eusebius's theology. Eusebius's depiction of Constantine's piety provides the background for Eusebius's interpretation of the Constantinian shift. When Constantine is portrayed as a pious person, it becomes easier for Eusebius to depict the Constantinian shift as a natural and positive change, which was in the interest of both the Roman Empire and the church. The way Eusebius describes Constantine's way to Christianity illustrates this better than anything else.

2.4.2.4 The Emperor's Embrace of Christianity

Why would a ruler like Constantine choose to become a Christian in the first place? According to Eusebius, Constantine weighed the different gods and deities against each other, and investigated which one he ought to follow to achieve success. Eusebius describes how Constantine decided that the Christian God was in fact the right God to follow based on the fact that his father, Constantius, had been successful and he allegedly had followed the Christian God.[67] According to Eusebius, Constantine realized that all the rulers who had followed "the multitude of Gods," all had come to various kinds of bitter ends, so it would be wise of him to choose differently.[68] Constantine chooses the God of victory. The reasoning behind Constantine choosing the Christian God is that it serves his own ends. The Christian God is by Constantine not perceived as an authority who determines what the goals of the empire and the emperor are to be. Does this mean that Eusebius depicts God as just a helper to Constantine? Not exactly. As we will see below, the *Vita Constantini*'s famous story of Constantine's vision before the battle at the Milvian Bridge (October 28, 312) shows what is God's plan and what is Constantine's plan, Eusebius understands to be tightly interwoven.

Eusebius can be quite dramatic in his account of the practical aspects of the emperor's new faith. The last remnants of Diocletian's Tetrarchy were still in place and Constantine's co-emperor Maxentius held Rome. Constantine marches from the north, Eusebius recounts, and plans to cross the

---

67. Constantine's father, Constantius, probably did not identify as Christian, but did adhere to some form of monotheistic religion. See Cameron and Hall, *Introduction and Commentaries*, 203.

68. *VC* I:27.1–3.

Milvian Bridge into Rome. But Maxentius summons his troops to meet him on the bridge. They gather on each side of the bridge and prepare for battle. But before the battle Constantine has a vision. He sees "with his own eyes, up in the sky and resting over the sun, a cross-shaped trophy formed from light, and a text attached to it which said, 'By this conquer.'"[69] On the following night Christ appears to Constantine in a dream and explains to him how he is to make a sign consisting of the first two letters of the word "Χριστός," a X vertically intersected by a P.[70] Constantine is instructed to fasten this symbol to an upright pole to carry with him into battle.[71] Of course "the Emperor who relied upon the support of God . . . overcame them all [Maxentius's armies] quite easily."[72]

What we see here is God depicted as coming to help the emperor to carry out what is from the outset the emperor's plan, which is also congruent with God's plan. God is understood to "stretch out his right hand to assist him [Constantine] in his plans."[73] Again it is seen that in Eusebius's interpretation, becoming a Christian does not alter the political goals of Constantine, but is interpreted as congruent with Constantine's political goals.

Eusebius tells that Constantine recounted his dream to him only a long while after it had occurred.[74] In connection to this event, Eusebius remarks that when it is taken into consideration how successful Constantine was to go on and become it is not to be doubted that the emperor really had this dream.[75] The criterion by which Eusebius judges that the dream was really from God is that Constantine later achieved success in matters of politics. Such an account reveals a specific interpretation of the relationship between God and the secular ruler. Does Eusebius think that Constantine achieved success because he believed in God? Not exactly.

69. *VC* I:28.2.
70. *VC* I:29–31.
71. This sign was to become known as the labarum; the Christian "battle-standard." See Cameron and Hall, *Introduction and Commentaries*, 207.
72. *VC* I:37.2.
73. *VC* I:28.1.
74. *VC* I:28.1.
75. Eusebius does not recount the story of the Vision of Constantine in the *Historia Ecclesiastica*. It is possible that Eusebius only did hear the history long after the battle, accounted by the emperor himself, as Eusebius states in I:28.1 of the *Vita Constantini*. It is more probable, though, that he added it to live up to the conventions of panegyric style. See Cameron and Hall, *Introduction and Commentaries*, 204–5.

His understanding is that the wish of what God and the emperor wanted to do in the world ran parallel to each other. Constantine did not change his plans to become ruler and gain political success because he became a Christian. But according to Eusebius that was not necessary either, since Constantine's personal ambition was already congruent with God's plan to establish a Christian empire. For Eusebius the Constantinian shift appeared as less of a shift, since the interest of the empire and the interest of the God were aligned. This was a point of view which could only be allowed for a writer who is in the very beginning of the Constantinian Era.

Augustine of Hippo shortly after came to learn more about how the interests of the secular ruler and the church did not always run parallel but more often could be pointing in very different directions. The relationship between even a Christian emperor and the church could often resemble more of the conflictual stroke of the χ than follow the harmonious swing of the ρ.

2.4.2.5 Violence Committed by the Emperor

When the interests of God and the secular ruler are perceived to be the same, a certain largesse in the methods applied to realize such interests is often observed. A largesse that often includes the use of violence. That is the case in the *Vita Constantini* too. Eusebius lauds how Constantine equipped his troops and "campaigned against the land of the Britons and the dwellers at the very Ocean where the sun sets."[76] He points out how Constantine "subdued" barbarian tribes and turned their savagery to gentleness, while he "repulsed and chased off his territory" other tribes.[77] And Eusebius describes how Constantine, when in 324 he won the battle against Licinius, his fellow Augustus, Constantine let enemy soldiers be "caught and killed according to the law of war."[78] That the emperor exerts violence in pursuits of plans to realize the will of God is not something which immediately troubles Eusebius. But then, during other parts of his account, Eusebius tries to depict Constantine as a merciful ruler, who does provide amnesty to his opponents, and allows them to flee: "…the Godbeloved [Constantine]

---

76. *VC* I:8.2.

77. *VC* I:25.1. The Greek word used for "subdue" is ὑποτάσσω. The word carries the quite violent meaning of forcing somebody to follow one's will.

78. *VC* II:10.2.

having instructed his men not to pursue hard, so that the fugitive [Licinius] might reach safety."[79]

Constantine is at the same time lauded by Eusebius for slaying his enemies and for showing mercy to his enemies. The *Vita Constantini* contains multiple of such opposite views on Constantine's exertion of violence, and in Eusebius's text they are allowed to remain unintegrated. That such two views of the exertion of violence can stand thus unintegrated reveals something important about Eusebius's interpretation of the Constantinian shift: It has a hard time accounting for what happens, when the interests of the empire and the interest of the church are not strictly aligned. Instead of attempting to negotiate how Constantine at the same time could be a victorious emperor, who was successful on the battlefield, and at the same time a pious Christian, who was forgiving and passionate, his understanding of the Constantinian shift does not allow for these two depictions of Constantine to come into conflict, and Eusebius has to let them stand un-negotiated.

Another instance of Constantine's exertion of violence is recounted by Eusebius when he describes how Constantine tore down Roman temples,[80] and sent out his men to dishonor the pagan priests and their gods: "[Constantine's men ordered] the consecrated officials themselves to bring out their gods with much mockery and contempt from their dark recesses, and then depriving them of their fine appearance and revealing to every eye the ugliness that lay within the superficially applied beauty."[81] This form of violence against another religious group does not seem to constitute a problem for Eusebius. Eusebius even recounts that Constantine prohibited "all those under Roman rule . . . every form of idolatry, and every form of sacrifice."[82] Had Eusebius deemed this way of treating adherents of other religions problematic, he would, in all probability, not have included it in the *Vita Constantini* at all. Here the historical evidence can help in understanding how Eusebius constructs the picture of Constantine. Cameron

---

79. *VC* II:11.1. In their commentary to the *Vita Constantini* Cameron and Hall state that many Christians still held to an original pacifism of Christianity, and Eusebius therefore had to describe Constantine as only reluctantly engaging in war. See Cameron and Hall, *Introduction and Commentaries*, 233–34. We will see in part 4 of this book that the question of how pacifist the early church was perceived can become a decisive factor for how the Constantinian shift is interpreted.

80. *VC* III:54.4–7.

81. *VC* III:54.6.

82. *VC* IV:23.

and Hall point out that in reality it was not Constantine's policy to ban pagan worship.[83] That means Eusebius has not only included, but actually gone out of the way to put extra stress on how Constantine persecuted adherents of other religions.

Earlier in the *Vita Constantini* Eusebius vividly narrated how Christians were persecuted.[84] Despite his laments over this prior persecution of Christians, Eusebius does not have a problem with depicting Constantine exerting force over people with different beliefs. That Eusebius does not take note of this is furthermore remarkable, as such a persecution would stand in conflict with the *Edict of Milan*. Here Constantine had granted "both to the Christians and to all men freedom to follow the religion which they choose" as Eusebius recounted it in his reference to the *Edict of Milan* in *Historia Ecclesiastica*.[85] Since the *Historia Ecclesiastica* was a work prior to the *Vita Constantini* it is to be presumed that Eusebius was acutely aware of how he is in the *Vita Constantini* portraying Constantine as not adhering to his own decree on this matter. How can it be that Eusebius can strongly criticize Christians being oppressed, while simultaneously depict Constantine as sanctioning the persecution of other religious groups? And, likewise, how can Eusebius laud the *Edict of Milan* and at the same time depict Constantine as not following it?

In the *Vita Constantini* Eusebius justifies Constantine's mistreatment of adherents of other religious groups by simply discounting their beliefs. What they believe in are not real gods, and the pagan religions are therefore not benefitting the empire. Since the gods in question are "false gods," it is good to persecute the people believing in them, due to the fact that following those gods does not lead to victory and progress for the empire. The Constantinian shift is by Eusebius interpreted as leading to progress for both the empire and the church, and the violence committed by the state then comes to flow naturally into the way the church acts.

What was it that led Eusebius to fail to recognize how his images of the pious Christian and the good emperor do not always align perfectly? What prevented him from seeing that slaughtering enemies and persecuting

---

83. Though Constantine presumably did not ban pagan worship it remains an open question as to whether pagan sacrifice was banned. In any case if such a ban really did exist, it was not strongly enforced at the time of Constantine. See Cameron and Hall, *Introduction and Commentaries*, 243.

84. See for example *VC* I:51.

85. *Historia Ecclesiastica* X:5.4.

adherents of other religions might not be congruent with a Christian ideal?[86] To answer this question it will be helpful to look at Eusebius's social location. Located at the top of the church leadership, Eusebius is on good terms with the secular ruler. He inhabits a social position in which there is not much danger that the violence exerted by Constantine will ever reach him. This social location probably influences how he interprets the Constantinian shift. Liberation Theology has brought such a hermeneutical principle into focus in the most telling manner by pointing out how privileged people, because of their perspective, often will experience difficulties in understanding most of the biblical stories.[87] Likewise, Eusebius's privileged social position inevitably structures and influences his account of the actions of the emperor. Eusebius's position makes it hard for him to recognize how the violence Constantine commits might constitute a problem for his portrayal as Constantine as a pious Christian. Eusebius is not forced to think about what it actually means when Constantine is slaughtering enemies or possibly persecuting adherents of other religions. That, I believe, can be the explanation Constantine's political deeds do not disturb Eusebius's picture of a harmonious relationship between the emperor and the ethics of the church, thus permitting Eusebius to interpret the Constantinian shift as church and empire aligned, as Eusebius is not confronted with the consequences of the so-called realpolitik.

2.4.3 *Theology and Politics*

2.4.3.1 THE CHRISTIAN MISSION

One remark from the *Vita Constantini*, though only said in passing, has gained special attention through history, when it comes to the question of the relationship between church and state.[88] Eusebius recounts how Constantine after the Council of Nicaea held a banquet for the bishops to

---

86. The ideal of absolute pacifism possibly belonged only to the very early church, but even the theology of the church in the fourth century did not condone outright killing and persecution.

87. "The idea of reading the text from a position of complete 'objectivity' is a myth constructed to protect the privileged space of those with the power to legitimize their interpretations." See De La Torre, *Reading the Bible from the Margins*, 37.

88. "In attempts to define the relations between the first Christian emperor and the Church, no phrase is more frequently quoted than this *obiter dictum*." See Seston, "Constantine as a 'Bishop,'" 127.

celebrate his *vicennalia*; his twentieth year of rule.[89] According to Eusebius, at this occasion Constantine let slip to the bishops that: "You are bishops of those within the Church, but I am perhaps a bishop appointed by God over those outside."[90] An aspect of Eusebius's theological model of the relationship between the church and the Roman Empire reveals itself here. Eusebius portrays Constantine as the ruler over all his people, including when it comes to religious affairs. Even though Constantine did not force people to become Christians in order to serve in the military or the government, Eusebius does portray him as having a pastoral vision for the whole population. However, this is a short passage and it cannot be seen as the only key to understanding Eusebius's interpretation of the relationship between church and empire.[91]

In Eusebius's interpretation of the Constantinian shift a number of core theological concepts have to be reinterpreted and accommodated to the new situation. If the short remark quoted above does not provide enough material for a thorough analysis of how this happens, then another topic will help fulfill this: Eusebius's understanding of mission. Eusebius portrays mission as something carried out by the emperor when he conquers new land. The empire conquering new land Eusebius understands as a way for the gospel to reach further out; even to "the end of the whole inhabited earth."[92] According to Eusebius, the rulers of the foreign lands were thankful and "spontaneously saluted and greeted him [Constantine]."[93] For Eusebius, these conquests are interpreted as a way for Constantine to announce the truth of God to the nations.[94] In Eusebius's interpretation of the Constantinian shift the concept of conquering new land and the concept of spreading Christianity becomes united. This conception of mission was later to become deeply grounded in Western modes of thought, but it is interesting to note how one of its first iterations is played out so vividly in the *Vita Constantini*.

---

89. *VC* III:15.1.

90. *VC* IV:24: ἀλλ' ὑμεῖς μὲν τῶν εἴσω τῆς ἐκκλησιας, ἐγὼ δὲ τῶν ἐκτὸς ὑπὸ θεοῦ καθεσταμένος ἐπίσκοπος ἂν εἴην. It has earlier been speculated that the οἵ ἐκτὸς should not mean those outside the church, and instead refer to the laity, see for example Seston, "Constantine as a 'Bishop'"; but more recent scholarship has rejected this idea, see Cameron and Hall, *Introduction and Commentaries*, 320.

91. Cameron and Hall, *Introduction and Commentaries*, 320.

92. *VC* I:8.4.

93. *VC* I:8.4.

94. Cameron and Hall, *Introduction and Commentaries*, 189.

In that sense Eusebius takes over the way religion was understood in the Roman Empire before the Constantinian shift. In his interpretation of the Constantinian shift the adoption of the Christian God as the protector of the empire did not mean that the general structures of society had to change. In Eusebius's interpretation Christianity did not lay claim on the empire to function differently once the Christian God had become its protector. For Eusebius Christianity could fill the role of the previous Roman religion, since God had wisely steered the course of history, so that Christianity could naturally fit in and take earlier Roman religion's place as the religion sustaining the empire.[95] In this lays a specific understanding of the course of history.

2.4.3.2 GOD IN CONTROL OF THE COURSE OF HISTORY

Eusebius's interpretation of the Constantinian shift is influenced by his theological framing of history. When reading the *Vita Constantini* it becomes clear that Eusebius sees history as progressing for the better. Contrary to the historiography of the early church, which did not have an unequivocal view on the development of history, Eusebius propagates a historiography of progress, wherein God continually reveals new wonders for the good of human beings.[96]

A number of examples from the *Vita Constantini* of how God intervenes and directs history can be given. The most striking example of Eusebius's depiction of God's steering of history is the example of how God removed the obstacles in the way for Constantine to become emperor of the whole Roman Empire. To make the historical events fall into place in this interpretation, Eusebius needs to portray Licinius, Constantine's fellow Augustus, brother-in-law, and later rival, as a morally corrupt enemy that God removed. Licinius had issued what was to become known as the *Edict of Milan* in unison with Constantine, and while Licinius did show openness toward Christianity, this fact is omitted by Eusebius. Instead Eusebius rhetorically sets up Licinius as a ruler with a bad moral standing, so that Eusebius can justify Constantine's war against him.[97] Only a year after

---

95. Even though Eusebius likes to depict Christianity quickly gaining popularity and paganism disappearing, that is not a historically accurate description, and paganism remained a vital force long after the Constantinian shift.

96. Chesnut, "Eusebius, Augustine, Orosius," 692.

97. Licinius was ambivalent toward Christianity throughout his life. When it was politically advantageous to him, he in fact turned against the church. See Barnes,

Constantine and Licinius had issued the *Edict of Milan*, as Augusti of the eastern and western part of the empire, they fell into the first of their conflicts. Ten years of hostility followed, but in 324 Constantine defeated Licinius.[98] Eusebius recounts how Licinius, before going into battle with Constantine, makes a speech to his soldiers, where he informs them that they are about to fight a traitor who has fallen to worship a foreign god. Eusebius then goes on to describe how Licinius understands this as a war between the old religion and the new religion.[99] Eusebius recognizes this too as a war between the old and the new religion, and Eusebius interprets the historical events as God directly intervening and giving victory to Constantine; thereby preparing the way for Constantine to create a Christian empire. When Licinius was stricken with illness, Eusebius calls it "a God-sent [θεόπεμπτος] punishment."[100] God is perceived as actively interfering in the political game, and Eusebius believes that it is possible to identify where and when God is at work. Thus, Eusebius views the Constantinian shift not only as a political occurrence, which happened to be in line with the plans God had for the world, but something directly brought about by God.

Eusebius's theology of God's intervention in history was more unequivocal than that of the early church, but also on other theological key areas did he see God as helping the emperor, as I will unfold below.

2.4.3.3 Baptism and Funeral

Eusebius's depiction of God steering the course of history in a way harmonious with Constantine's interests leads back to the question of Eusebius's understanding of Constantine's personal relationship to Christianity. Today, infant baptism, in many Christian confessions, is considered the starting place for the Christian life. Earlier scholarly literature on Constantine stressed the fact that Constantine did not get baptized until the end of his

---

Constantine and Eusebius, 70. But this ambiguity is not mentioned in the *Vita Constantini*, as it was a part of Eusebius's literary strategy to "silence" Licinius, and portray him in opposition to Constantine. See Cameron and Hall, *Introduction and Commentaries*, 323.

98. Barnes, *Constantine and Eusebius*, 76.
99. *VC* II:5.
100. *VC* I:57.1. Divine intervention can apparently take on a repulsive form: "A general inflammation arose in the middle of his bodily [i.e., Licinius's] private parts, then a deeply fistulous ulcer; these spread incurably to his intestines, from which an unspeakable number of maggots bred and a stench of death arose" (I:57.2).

life; and interpreted this to mean that he was not a Christian until late in his life, maybe only at his deathbed. However, infant baptism was not common in Constantine's time and "despite what has often been imagined, Constantine's late baptism carries no implication the Emperor was unsure of his faith."[101] Eusebius recounts Constantine's expressed desire to be baptized in the River Jordan, but that it was only up to God to decide to whom to grant such an honor.[102]

Among all Eusebius's references to initiation, purified rebirth and brightness in the baptismal account, one remark is of particular interest to this book. Eusebius mentions that after his baptism, Constantine put on the bright baptismal clothes and was "unwilling to touch a purple robe again."[103] The purple robe was the imperial robe associated with the office of the emperor.[104] Eusebius thereby implies that when Constantine was fully initiated as a Christian, he did not want to take care of the imperial obligations any longer. The historicity of these events is unreliable,[105] but what Eusebius presumably wants to express with this remark purvey a clear image; here Eusebius sees a problem in an absolute union of worldly power and Christianity. Even though throughout the *Vita Constantini* Eusebius lauds the emperor as a Godsend and the benefactor of the Christian church, he still hesitates to unify completely the office of the emperor with a Christian

---

101. Cameron and Hall, *Introduction and Commentaries*, 341.

102. *VC* IV:62.2. The story of Constantine's baptism soon became material for a number of legends and alternative versions started to appear. According to the *Actus Sylvestri* from the fifth century, Pope Sylvester baptized Constantine in Rome. This story later came to provide the narrative background for the Donation of Constantine. See Cameron and Hall, *Introduction and Commentaries*, 341. According to a more colorful account, Sylvester and the chief Rabbi of Rome had a contest in the Coliseum. A bull was struck dead when the rabbi whispered the secret name of God; but was resurrected in the name of Christ by Sylvester. For Constantine this served as evidence of the power of the Christian God and Constantine was subsequently baptized. See Drake, *Constantine and the Bishops*, 394–95.

103. *VC* IV:62.5.

104. The purple was seen as the symbol of the office of the emperor to such an extent that when the emperor was lying in state before his funeral, the people paid tribute not by kissing the body but by kissing the purple robe, as this epitomized the office of the emperor. See Avery, "Adoratio Purpurae," 72–73. The purple was later the color worn by bishops when acting as judges. Yet an example of how the Constantinian shift affected both church and empire and subsequently led the church to adopt the symbolic language of the Roman Empire.

105. Cameron and Hall, *Introduction and Commentaries*, 342.

life.[106] That Eusebius is not willing to let the identity of emperor and the identity as a Christian fully conflate in his depiction of Constantine, reveals how Eusebius's interpretation is informed not only by what would suit the emperor, but also by a theological perspective.

It can be concluded that Eusebius does not embrace a complete unification of the Christian church and the secular powers, at least not in the way it was laid out in much earlier scholarship. That Eusebius resists unifying completely the image of the emperor and the image of the pious Christian testifies to the theological nature of Eusebius's work, since had he been just a sycophant, he would presumably have had no problem in completely merging the church and the secular powers. Eusebius does argue that these are aligned, but it must be acknowledged that he does not claim a complete merging.

Eusebius's description of Constantine's funeral arrangement further illustrates this lack of a complete merger. Eusebius here skillfully communicates at the same time the distinction between the Roman Empire and the Christian religion and maintains what Christianity can offer the empire. Eusebius describes how what used to be a pagan service was replaced by a Christian funeral service, but with central elements of the old ritual still maintained. Eusebius describes how Constantine first was lying-in-state at the palace, thereafter to be carried to the mausoleum he had built for himself at the Church of the Holy Apostles in Constantinople.[107] Instead of the traditional imperial funeral pyre, Constantine was inhumed, but the tradition of honoring the emperor that had taken place as part of the pagan rite, was still maintained.[108]

The crucial aspect here is that Eusebius is not attempting to replace the old funeral ritual with a new one. He is not trying to adapt and change old rituals into a new Christian ritual.[109] Instead Eusebius is conveying the message that the old, the imperial rule with all its customs, and the new, the Christian faith, are coming together harmoniously. In conclusion the imagery from the coin described in section 2.4.2.2 can be drawn to attention

---

106. Cameron and Hall argue that "this change [Constantine's baptism] involves attaching himself to the intimacy of the worship he is now allowed to join, and accepting moral standards, which certainly for many Christians, and perhaps even for Eusebius, were not thought compatible with the military and civil duties and worldly commitments of an emperor." See Cameron and Hall, *Introduction and Commentaries*, 342.

107. *VC* IV:60.3; IV:66–70.

108. Cameron and Hall, *Introduction and Commentaries*, 347.

109. Cameron and Hall, *Introduction and Commentaries*, 349.

again. God and Constantine are by Eusebius understood to be reaching for each other. Eusebius's understanding of the Constantinian shift does not entail Eusebius conceding a theological approach. Eusebius's understanding of the Constantinian shift is sustained by a theological vision of how God's plan for the world and Constantine's ambitions in unison lead to the creation of the Christian Roman Empire.

Eusebius's thinking is indeed theological, and it is exactly the theological nature of his historical account which makes it possible to compare the *Vita Constantini* to other theological accounts of the Constantinian shift arising centuries later. Though, as I will look into over the next pages, the theological nature of his writing was forgotten by the scholarly world for a while.

2.5 The Contemporary Debate

Here I will first lay out how a change has taken place within contemporary scholarship on Eusebius and then I will venture an explanation as to what prevented modern scholarship from a proper reading of Eusebius.

2.5.1 A Renewed Interest in Eusebius

Despite the theological character of his writing, Eusebius has tended to draw more attention as a source for historians of early Christianity and the Roman Empire than as a writer and a thinker in his own right. Within earlier scholarship, it was customary to interpret Eusebius as succumbing theological interest to political interest—to argue that Eusebius was taken by surprise by the swiftness of the Constantinian shift, and simply yielded to pleasing the worldly powers.[110] Here we will first look at how Eusebius was treated in earlier scholarship and then turn the attention to the change in newer scholarship on Eusebius.

Michael Hollerich points out how the picture of Eusebius in early modern scholarship was muddled as he was at the same time characterized both as "a political propagandist, a good courtier, the shrewd and worldly adviser of the Emperor Constantine, the great publicist of the first Christian emperor, the first in a long succession of ecclesiastical politicians, the herald of Byzantinism, a political theologian, a political metaphysician,

---

110. Penner, "Rhetoric of God in History," 5–6.

and a caesaropapist."[111] For example, Jacob Burckhardt (1818–1897) famously referred to Eusebius as "the first thoroughly dishonest historian of antiquity."[112] Burckhardt believed that Eusebius's deceptive way of describing Constantine as an overly pious person blurred the picture of Constantine, so that his political genius was never properly acknowledged. Another example is Jean Sirinelli (1921–2004), who claimed that Eusebius blatantly collapsed the understanding of the first coming of Christ with the eschatological second coming of Christ, with the goal of being able to speak highly about Constantine and the great success of the church.[113]

Seldom, though, was Eusebius read on his own terms and not just as a source utilized to answer other questions. Often Eusebius, and the *Vita Constantini* especially, was read with the aim of casting light on biographical questions of whether Constantine really converted. A new interest in Constantine is to a lesser extent preoccupied with Constantine's personal biography, but instead turns the attention toward questions of the broader political implications of Constantine's reign.[114] Such a different interest in Constantine has opened up other ways of approaching and evaluating the works of Eusebius. Let us turn to this new reading of Eusebius.

In her 2011 published monograph titled *Reconsidering Eusebius*, Sabrina Inowlocki thus characterizes the change in the reading of Eusebius: "New light has been shed both on his writings and on his personality, which has led to a welcome re-assessment of his significance. The influence of post-modern studies has contributed to see Eusebius as an active participant in the construction of late antique history, theology, and literature."[115] But only within the last thirty years or so have this change taken place. Averil Cameron and Michael J. Hollerich are contemporary voices, who have critiqued the earlier approach to Eusebius's work. Cameron, coauthor

111. Hollerich, "Religion and Politics in the Writings of Eusebius," 309.

112. Burckhardt, *Age of Constantine the Great*, 283. "Er [Eusebius] ist aber der erste durch und durch unredliche Geschichtsschreiber des Altertums." The German wording is here cited from *Die Kirche angesichts der konstantinischen Wende*. See Ruhbach, "Die politische Theologie Eusebs von Caesarea," 238.

113. Sirinelli, *Les vues historiques d'Eusèbe de Césarée durant la période prénicéenne*, *Publications de la Section de Langues et Littératures*, 484–85. For an elaborate list of proponents of this old reading of Eusebius, see Hollerich, "Religion and Politics in the Writings of Eusebius," 309–10.

114. For an overview of recent developments in contemporary studies on Constantine, see the section "'Out of the Mist': The Current State of Constantinian Studies," in Thompson, "From Sinner to Saint?," 5–9.

115. Inowlocki and Zamagni, *Reconsidering Eusebius*, viii–ix.

to the translation and commentary on the *Vita Constantini* used on the previous pages, formulates the critique of the earlier reading of Eusebius this way: "it is one thing to admit that Eusebius passionately believed in the rightness of his own vision, and quite another to claim that the Life was a documentary history, a sober and accurate account of 'what really happened.' Such a description would be just as untrue of the *Historia Ecclesiastica*, Eusebius's other main 'historical' work. If ever there was an author unsuited to a positivist critique, that author is Eusebius."[116] In German scholarship, already in the seventies Gerhard Ruhbach pointed out how Eusebius was first and foremost a theologian, who addressed political and historical questions as part of his theological work.[117] But most poignantly Timothy Barnes's seminal work *Constantine and Eusebius* (1981) challenged the old interpretation of Eusebius by pointing out that Eusebius is a theologian in his own right and that it is the church and not the empire, which is the ultimate eschatological goal for him. Barnes located Eusebius's understanding of the emperor within a specific vision of the progression of political development; a vision guided by theological concerns.[118]

The perspectives on Eusebius's work opened up by this new approach are especially interesting for this book. Eusebius was not just pleasing Constantine, or his sons, but was guided by a theological vision. Thus these new approaches to Eusebius that deal with Eusebius in his own right as a theological historian support the analysis of the *Vita Constantini* presented above.

2.5.2 Theological History-Writing

It can seem obvious that Eusebius's *Vita Constantini* should be read not strictly as historical but rather as theological history-writing—especially when taking into consideration what Eusebius explicitly says about this issue in the *Vita Constantini*.[119] By masterful stylistic application of a periodic

---

116. Cameron, "Eusebius' *Vita Constantini*," 154–55.

117. "Sein eigentliches Interesse ist aber auch in seiner letzten Schrift [*Vita Constantini*] kirchlich-theologisch orientiert." See Ruhbach, "Die politische Theologie Eusebs von Caesarea," 250.

118. For an elaborate account of the development of this new approach to Eusebius, see Hollerich, "Religion and Politics in the Writings of Eusebius," 312–13.

119. One could suggest a differentiation between Eusebius's works to be made, arguing that the *Historia Ecclesiastica* is intended as a historical work, whereas the *Vita Constantini* is more a piece of theological writing. However, the new approach to Eusebius

sentence, Eusebius makes very clear that he is less interested in actually describing the historical facts: "The greatest, the imperial parts of the history of the Thriceblessed [Constantine], his encounters and battles in war, his valiant deeds and victories and routing of enemies, and how many triumphs he won, his peacetime decrees for the welfare of the state and the benefit of the individual, and the legal enactments which he imposed for the improvement of the life of his subjects, and most of his other acts as Emperor, and those which everybody remembers, I intend to omit."[120] Eusebius thereby early in the *Vita Constantini* spells out that he is in fact not writing what today would be understood as a strict work of history intended to purvey a full historical account of what happened. Eusebius's *Vita Constantini* is not attempting to portray Constantine "historically correct," but rather to provide a theological interpretation of the Constantinian shift, which depicts the interests of the church and the Roman Empire as aligned with each other.

Why is it then, when Eusebius clearly says that he is not interested in purveying a minute historical account, that from at least the nineteenth century and till around the 1980s he was read and criticized as a bad historian? What was it in the approach of historians, which did not allow for the works of Eusebius to be read as the theological history-writing they are? The answer to this question pertains to general questions of the relationship between church history and theology relevant for this book.

To read Eusebius properly requires an understanding of the relationship between politics and theology in a way that has not been prevalent within theology for at least the last two hundred years. Scholars have understood Eusebius to address religion from a political point of view, when it is in reality the other way around. Eusebius did not just baptize the political but had a theology that naturally had a political side to it.[121] As also the Swedish theologian Arne Rasmussen has pointed out, there is an important difference between "political theology," which is predominantly governed by a materialistic worldview and wants to gain political influence, and "theological politics," which operates with a grander metaphysical ontology

---

does not operate with such distinctions. See Barnes, *Constantine and Eusebius*, 126–28.

120. *VC* I:11.1.

121. Hollerich spells this out very clearly: "History, and therefore politics, was assessed from a religious standpoint, and not the other way around. The difference is important, but scholars have not always respected it." See Hollerich, "Religion and Politics in the Writings of Eusebius," 324.

that also has a political aspect to it.[122] Eusebius wrote within the last category. But this way of writing history made it difficult for modern scholars to understand what he was doing, as this is not the way theological writing is most often conceived today.

Recent development within theology points out that the idea of a sharp distinction between, on the one side, an understanding of history and politics that is guided by theology and, on the other side, an understanding of history that is not guided by a theology, might be a delusion in the first place. As William Cavanaugh has made clear in his book *Theopolitical Imagination* there is no such thing as a concept of history or politics, which is not also theological. The vocabulary used in political language clearly reveals this.[123] It is a misconception born out of parts of Enlightenment thought that it is possible to operate with a concept of a political or historical account, which is at the same time not also theological.[124] Since a historical account is operating with concepts of the purpose and the direction of human history it will by necessity have a theological aspect to it.

An awareness of this connection between theology and politics will prove helpful also for the analysis of Augustine and Yoder. Now first let me sum up the previous sections on Eusebius's interpretations of the Constantinian shift.

2.6 Conclusion

Wolfhart Pannenberg in his *Systematische Theologie* points out that people who believe Christianity to have a political responsibility should not be so quick in judging Eusebius, as he was one of the founding theologians for accounting theologically for the political responsibility of the church.[125] On the previous pages we have seen that theology played out. Eusebius did have a theology for what he was doing in his writing of the *Vita Constantini* and was not just a sycophant. Contrary to how Eusebius's work was depicted in

---

122. See Rasmussen, *Church as Polis*.

123. This is an insight, which was re-introduced into contemporary scholarship by German jurist and philosopher Carl Schmitt (1880–1985). See for example Schmitt, *Politische Theologie*.

124. See Cavanaugh, *Theopolitical Imagination*; and Bretherton, *Christianity and Contemporary Politics*.

125. "Wer die politische Verantwortung des Christentums in der jeweils gegenwärtigen Situation betont, sollte jedenfalls weniger leichtfertig und abfällig über Euseb urteilen als das wethin üblich geworden ist." See Pannenberg, *Systematische Theologie*, 519.

earlier scholarship we saw that Eusebius was driven by a theological vision, which provided a theological account for the changed circumstances of the church after the ascendance of a Christian emperor. The central tenets in Eusebius's interpretation of the Constantinian shift can be summed up in five points. (a) Eusebius was not a sycophant who just wanted to appease the emperor, but was driven by a theological vision, which formed his interpretation of the Constantinian shift. (b) This theological vision dictated that with the Constantinian shift the interests of the secular ruler and the interests of God aligned harmoniously. That meant the church ought not to separate itself from the rest of society, but could contribute to the common good by influencing how the empire was ruled. (c) According to Eusebius the Constantinian shift was thereby not just a political occurrence, but rather the culmination of a historical development, in line with Eusebius understanding of history as moving forward. (d) This implied that God's action in the course of history could actually be identified, and Eusebius clearly identified God's actions in the Constantinian shift. (e) For Eusebius the Constantinian shift therefore served as evidence that it will eventually go Christians well in this world, and the Roman Empire was the locus for this eschatological realization.

Having established that Eusebius's work was in fact governed by a theological vision is a statement on the nature of his work, not a statement of whether he was right in his theological assessment of the relationship between church and empire. But only when having established that the *Vita Constantini* is a theological work, can it be properly understood and compared to other theological interpretations of the Constantinian shift. Eusebius's depiction of the Constantinian shift entailed a new interpretation of key theological concepts, as Eusebius at the same time had to hold together the image of the good emperor and the image of the pious Christian in one man. This feat could not be accomplished without Eusebius addressing such theological concepts as ecclesiology, questions of war, and eschatology. Core matters that Augustine and Yoder interpreted in a different manner.

Eusebius's interpretation of the Constantinian shift came about in a time when both the church and the empire experienced progress, and this context played a role for the way Eusebius came to interpret the Constantinian shift. But in 413, only seventy-four years after the death of Eusebius, the situation had changed dramatically. The empire was weakened by the sack of Rome by the vandals in 410 and the church experienced internal quarrels. In the midst of this upheaval, another bishop, this time from North Africa, was to lay out a different model for how to interpret the Constantinian shift.

Part III:

A Corrective

3

Augustine of Hippo

3.1 Introduction

The first chapter of Gerard O'Daly's readers guide to *De Civitate Dei* is concerned not with Augustine of Hippo (354–430), but instead provides a long account of Constantine and Eusebius.[1] Such a compositional choice in the layout of a guide to the *De Civitate Dei* reveals something about the theological context in which Augustine wrote his large work. In the *De Civitate Dei* Augustine is reacting against the kind of interpretation of the Constantinian shift that finds expression in the *Vita Constantini*. Augustine was writing in a context in which Eusebius's manner of interpreting the Constantinian shift had been deeply formative for the understanding of the relationship between the church and the Roman Empire, but Augustine presents a profoundly different interpretation of the Constantinian shift.[2] How this interpretation came to expression in the *De Civitate Dei*, and how it compares to that of the *Vita Constantini*, is what I will look at in this part 3 of the book.[3]

---

1. O'Daly, *Augustine's City of God*, 1–8.
2. Glenn Chesnut finds it necessary to utilize combat imagery to properly describe what Augustine was doing: "If we look back over the centuries from our present standpoint, it is clear that Eusebius was the great founding father of the complex of ideas that Augustine was attacking, and it is by referring to Eusebius that we see its theological, philosophical, and psychological underpinnings—fundamental ideas that Augustine had to modify or refute in order to establish his own, new interpretation of history." See Chesnut, "Pattern of the Past," 70–71.
3. A note on translations of the *De Civitate Dei* is appropriate here. The three main

I will begin with a short comparison to Eusebius's context; that I have labeled the differences in "exterior" matters (pertaining to location and time).[4] The next section will be an analysis of Augustine's interpretation of the Constantinian shift as expressed in the *De Civitate Dei* with special attention to book 19. This analysis makes it possible to arrive at a preliminary conclusion on Augustine's interpretation of the Constantinian shift. Then I will engage a highly relevant debate within contemporary scholarship on Augustine, particularly pertaining to his evaluation of the secular. This all renders possible a comparison between Eusebius and Augustine and their interpretation of the Constantinian shift, which will be labeled the "interior" differences (pertaining to theology).

3.2 Augustine and Eusebius (Exterior Differences)

"World empires were monuments to human selfishness, Augustine said."[5] As this quotation suggests, and as it will become evident in the subsequent sections, Augustine and Eusebius did not interpret the Constantinian shift

---

English scholarly translations of the *De Civitate Dei* are Marcus Dods's translation (originally published 1887 as *The City of God*), Henry Bettenson's translation (originally published 1972 as *Concerning the City of God Against the Pagans*), and Robert W. Dyson's translation (published 1998 as *The City of God Against the Pagans*). For English quotations I have relied on Dyson's work, since (or despite the fact that) he, in his own words, has "sacrificed elegance to accuracy." See Augustine, *City of God Against the Pagans*, xv. I have made comparisons to the two other translations where appropriate. For quotations of the Latin text I have used Dombart and Kalb's 4th critical edition of *De Civitate Dei* (originally published 1928–1929). The 4th edition of Dombart and Kalb used in this book is published by French scholar Gustave Combès and therefore differs in regard to punctuation from the American Loeb edition, though the Latin text is identical. Dombart and Kalb's 4th critical edition provides the best available Latin text; see O'Daly, *Augustine's City of God*, 276; and both Bettenson and Dyson base their translation on this edition. New City Press has in 2017 finished the publication of a complete English translation of the works of Augustine, which is expected to take the place as the new standard English translation of his work.

4. A vigilant reader might at this point feel a certain nervousness. What number of qualifying paragraphs will need to be written in part 4, in order to establish a conversation between interpretations of the Constantinian shift separated by around sixteen hundred years? The reader can rest assured, though, that this final comparison of the historiography of the Constantinian shift will be on a structural level, which will not necessitate the same form of qualifying historical leveling. Furthermore, the reader ought instead to feel content, due to the demonstrated understanding of exactly where we are now in the progression of the book.

5. Chesnut, "Pattern of the Past," 92.

quite the same way. When attempting to understand how these two bishops could interpret the Constantinian shift so differently, a look into the context of the two is not irrelevant. As mentioned on the first pages of this book, questions of the relationship between church and state fall into the category of theological questions, where a "timeless answer" cannot be given, and the questions of context gain extra importance.[6] Here I will look into how what could be labeled the "exterior" background of Augustine differs from that of Eusebius. I will first look into what separates them in regard to time and then what separates them in regard to location.

3.2.1 *Different Time*

Eusebius and Augustine were born almost a hundred years apart and both died in their mid-to-late seventies.[7] These intervening hundred years were a very eventful period in the history of the Roman Empire, and this historical change came to be formative for Augustine's understanding of the Constantinian shift. As described in the preceding section, Eusebius wrote in a context of progress for both the Roman Empire and the church. This context had changed in the time of Augustine. That Augustine wrote under very different circumstances becomes immediately obvious when comparing the factors that motivated the *Vita Constantini* and the *De Civitate Dei*, respectively. The *Vita Constantini* lauded the emperor and celebrated the Christianization of the Roman Empire—something that stands in a stark

---

6. To draw a distinction between what is contextual theology and what is not contextual theology may be an unsustainable position altogether. As catholic theologian Stephen Bevans has pointed out, all theology is essentially contextual: "Classical theology conceived theology as a kind of objective science of faith. It was understood as a reflection on faith on the two *loci theologici* (theological sources) of scripture and tradition, the content of which has not and never will be changed, and is above culture and historically conditioned expression. But what makes contextual theology precisely contextual is the recognition of the validity of another *locus theologicus*: present human experience. Theology that is contextual realizes that culture, history, contemporary thought forms, and so forth are to be considered. And so today we speak of theology as having *three* sources or *loci theologici*: scripture, tradition, and present human experience—or context." See Bevans, *Models of Contextual Theology*, 3–4. It is worth noting, though, that Bevans still operates with scripture and tradition as theological *loci* different from human experience or context. The context is certainly not the only source to be considered when pondering a theological question; but in regard to a theological investigation of the question of the relationship between church and state it is a factor, which cannot be dismissed.

7. Eusebius of Caesarea lived ca. 260–339, whereas Augustine of Hippo lived 354–430.

contrast to what Augustine in the *Retractationes* lays out as prompting him to begin writing *De Civitate Dei* in 413.[8]

Augustine explains how it was the sack of Rome in 410 by the (Arian Christian) Gothic king Alaric, which gave occasion to commencing the *De Civitate Dei*.[9] The sack of Rome led the worshippers of the traditional Roman gods to argue that this defeat could happen only because Rome had abandoned its traditional gods, and these critics thereby blamed the misfortune of Rome on the shift of faith to the Christian God. Such ideas also made their way to Hippo, which had taken a large number of refugees from Rome. Augustine did not agree to this view, and in his sermons from 410 and 411 he preached against the view that the fall of Rome had to do with the fact that the Roman Empire had turned Christian. He had thereby developed what later was to become the main themes of the *De Civitate Dei*.[10] Whereas Eusebius was conducting a theological interpretation of the Constantinian shift in a time when Christianity was welcomed by the Roman elite, Augustine was writing during a time when Christianity was under attack from the Roman elite. Such a difference in attitude toward the church was bound to influence Augustine's interpretation of the Constantinian shift. As it will be revealed in the next sections, such a shift in the attitude of the Roman elite helped to unveil for Augustine how the interest of the church and the empire were not always congruent.

3.2.2 *Different Location*

Not only did Eusebius and Augustine live in different times, but they were also situated differently both in regard to social and geographical location.

---

8. Augustine's *Retractationes* is not a work in which Augustine takes back what he has written, but a critical retrospect, where he is going over 93 of his works. In the prologue of *Retractationes* he describes his undertaking this way: "*Iam diu est, ut facere cogito atque dispono quod nunc, adiuvante domino, aggredior, quia differendum esse non arbitror, ut opuscula mea sive in libris sive in epistolis sive in tractatibus cum quadam iudiciaria severitate recenseam et, quod me offendit, velut censoris stilo denotem.*" ("For a long time I have been thinking about and planning to do something which I, with God's assistance, am now undertaking because I do not think it should be postponed: with a kind of judicial severity, I am reviewing my works—books, letters, and sermons—and, as it were, with the pen of a censor, I am indicating what dissatisfies me." Translated in Augustine, *Retractions.*)

9. Even though Augustine began writing the *De Civitate Dei* in 413, he did not finish it before 427; see O'Daly, *Augustine's City of God*, 34–35.

10. O'Daly, *Augustine's City of God*, 28–29.

Even though the exact character of Eusebius's relationship to Constantine is a debated issue, it is a fact that Eusebius was located geographically closer to the center of power than Augustine. Hippo Regius, where Augustine was consecrated bishop around 395, was by no means an insignificant city.[11] It bordered the Mediterranean and stood in immediate contact with the rest of the Roman Empire. But after the weakening of the western part of the Roman Empire, it found itself removed from the political center. Hippo Regius was located so far west that the influence of classical Greek language and culture was much less prevalent than in Caesarea, which led Augustine to draw inspiration primarily from classical Latin sources.[12] In the very year of Augustine's death (430) the city was sacked by the vandals. Even though Augustine can hardly be labelled a "voice from the margins," his distance to the center of power did allow him the possibility of developing an interpretation of the Constantinian shift more critical toward the rulers of the empire. Even the genre of the two works can serve to exemplify this. Whereas the *Vita Constantini* falls close to a panegyric in genre, the *De Civitate Dei* is written in an apologetic style. Augustine's context, specifically his more remote position, both socially and geographically, thereby came to have an influence on his interpretation of the Constantinian shift.

Throughout the *De Civitate Dei* Augustine did not shy away from preliminary remarks, before moving to the core of the matter. These detours were a necessity for him, though, as he was drawing up a whole new theological model for interpreting history. It is my hope that these prefatory remarks on the exterior differences between Eusebius and Augustine has not only been a detour but served as an inroad into Augustine's rather different interpretation of the Constantinian shift.

3.3 Augustine's Interpretation of the Constantinian Shift

The Trappist monk Thomas Merton has said of the *De Civitate Dei* that it can be considered the autobiography of the Catholic Church.[13] If that is

---

11. Hippo Regius is in ruins today, but was located on the outskirts of present-day Annaba in the northeastern part of present-day Algeria.

12. Though Augustine was not unable to read Greek, he never got a good hold on the language, and he read Eusebius in Jerome's Latin translation; see O'Daly, *Augustine's City of God*, 184.

13. "The autobiography of the Catholic Church. That is what *The City of God* is. Just as truly as the *Confessions* are the autobiography of St. Augustine, *The City of God* is the autobiography of the Church written by the most Catholic of her great saints." From

true it should come as no surprise that the *De Civitate Dei* is a large work. Even Augustine multiple places apologized for the length of his books.[14] Due to the magnitude of the work I cannot carry through an investigation of the interpretation of the Constantinian shift throughout all of the *De Civitate Dei*.[15] What is possible, though, is a focused analysis of parts of the work where Augustine conveys his reinterpretation of the Constantinian shift. That of course comes to expression most poignantly in his theology of the two cities. Augustine's way of writing is characterized by introducing, reintroducing and reiterating his main themes multiple times. The theme of the two cities Augustine treats in such a manner too. The theme is developed throughout the *De Civitate Dei*, but it is spelled out most clearly in book 19.[16]

What I will do here is first to give an outline of the *De Civitate Dei* and then move on to analyze how Augustine's interpretation of the Constantinian shift comes to expression in book 19. The third and last part of this section 3.3 will consist in a thematic reading focusing on themes pertaining to the Constantinian shift addressed elsewhere in *De Civitate Dei*. James J. O'Donnell has referred to the *De Civitate Dei* as "the longest single work presenting a sustained argument unified around a coherent single theme to survive from Greco-Roman antiquity."[17] Even though it might be unified around a single theme it still picks up many different arguments along the way. In order to get an overview of the work it will be appropriate to

---

Thomas Merton's introduction to the 1950 Random House publication of Dods's translation of the *De Civitate Dei*. See Augustine, *City of God*, xvii.

14. See for example *ciu.* IV:34 and XVII:24—when referencing the *De Civitate Dei* I refer to book and chapter with Roman numerals denoting the book of the *De Civitate Dei* and Arabic numerals denoting the chapter.

15. Augustine ends the *De Civitate Dei* with yet a comment on the length of his work. Translated with rhetorical finesse by Bettenson: "And now, as I think, I have discharged my debt, with the completion, by God's help, of this huge work. It may be too much for some, too little for others. Of both these groups I ask forgiveness. But of those for whom it is enough I make this request: that they do not thank me, but join with me in rendering thanks to God. Amen. Amen" (*ciu.* XXII:30).

16. The theme of the two cities is not only developed throughout the *De Civitate Dei*, but aspects of this line of though is also to be found in Augustine's sermons from around 410 and in *De Vera Religione*, *De Catechizandis Rudibus* and in *De Genesesi ad Litteram*. It is a fact, though, that the theme of the two cities is only fully unfolded in the *De Civitate Dei*. See O'Daly, *Augustine's City of God*, 265–66.

17. O'Donnell, "Augustine, *City of God*."

begin with an outline, in order to help direct attention to where Augustine is touching on matters pertaining to the Constantinian shift.[18]

First of all, one needs to be aware of an important structural shift of the work between book 10 and book 11. The first 10 books are written apologetically *contra paganos* and are composed in the manner of Cicero with the mastery of form and content of the classical world. From book 11 to the end, by book 22, Augustine reverts to a humbler style in order to expound an ecclesiastical message, which lays out a counterproposal to the pagan conception of history.[19] This rhetorical shift serves as a signpost: The second part of the work will be most relevant for the question of how Augustine interprets the Constantinian shift.

The first five books are characterized by Augustine's question "where were the gods"? In these books Augustine surveys the moral decay of Roman religion, and strives to show that military success and failure is not dependent on the observance or neglect of Roman religious practices. There were military and societal failures also at the time when Rome only worshipped its traditional gods.[20] If success is not dependent of worship of Roman gods, it begs the question why it should be so in regard to worship of the Christian God? In chapter 25 of book 5 Augustine comments on Constantine, and points out that Constantine's success was not due to the fact that he was a Christian, as God has allowed success to pagan emperors like Julian too. Thus, from the beginning of the *De Civitate Dei* the deviation from Eusebius's account of the Constantinian shift is clear.

In books 6 to 10 Augustine sets out to describe how Roman religious beliefs are ineffectual in relation to the afterlife, and only minor chapters in book 6 are of relevance for the question of Augustine's interpretation of the Constantinian shift.

The end of book 10 marks the close of the part of the work preoccupied with the refutations of wrong beliefs.[21] Augustine has now finished refuting the critics, who turned against Christianity after the sack of Rome

---

18. For the categorization of the books of the *De Civitate Dei* I have found inspiration in the main structure of Gerard O'Daly's outline; see O'Daly's *Augustine's City of God*, vii. O'Daly's book has received much appraisal as it covers the need for a readers guide to the *De Civitate Dei* and makes "sober judgment based on expert knowledge and diligent scholarship." See Pollmann, review of *Augustine's City of God: A Reader's Guide*, 971. For a slightly different categorization of the books of the *De Civitate Dei*, see the introduction to Bettenson's translation *Concerning the City of God against the Pagans*, xxxvii–xxxviii.

19. O'Donnell, "Augustine, *City of God*."

20. O'Daly, *Augustine's City of God*, 80.

21. O'Daly, *Augustine's City of God*, 135.

in 410, and can proceed to unfold his interpretation of how to conceive of the relationship between the Roman Empire and Christianity. He begins to unfold in detail the theory of the two cities. In books 11–14 Augustine recounts the origin of the two cities. He explains how the Fall was of such magnitude that it changed the nature of human being so that it would have led everyone to the "second death to which there is no end."[22] But by his unmerited love God extended his grace. This intervention led to the creation of two groups of people. Augustine says about these two groups that even though there are a great many nations throughout the world, all with their various languages, customs and dresses; there "exist only two orders, as we may call them, of human society [*societas*][23] and, following our Scriptures,[24] we may rightly speak of these as two cities. The one is made up of men who live according to the flesh, and the other of those who live according to the spirit."[25] The inhabitants of these two "cities" are united by their love either for the earthly pleasures or for the heavenly reward. In book 14 Augustine puts it this way: "Two cities, then, have been created by two loves: that is, the earthly by love of self extending even to contempt of God, and the heavenly by love of God extending the contempt of self."[26] In relation to Augustine's interpretation of the Constantinian shift it is of importance to clarify that these *societas* or cities are not to be understood as physically distinct institutions. They cannot be immediately equaled with church and secular society, respectively.[27]

22. ciu. XIV:1: "*secundam . . . mortem, cuius nullus est finis.*"

23. The semantic range of the word *societas* spans from fellowship or association to alliance or confederacy. Augustine does thereby not depict the two cities as physical entities, but rather as two communities tied together by their love either for the earthly or for the heavenly. See *societas* in Lewis and Short, *Latin Dictionary*.

24. Augustine is probably referring to Eph 2:19–22 and Phil 3:17–21. See Augustine, *City of God against the Pagans*, 260.

25. ciu. XIV:1: "*non tamen amplius quam duo quaedam genera humanae societatis existerent, quas civitates duas secundum scripturas nostras merito appellare possemus. Una quippe est hominum secundum carnem, altera secundum spiritum vivere in sui cuiusque generis pace volentium.*"

26. ciu. XIV:28: "*Fecerunt itaque civitates duas amores duo, terrenam scilicet amor sui usque ad contemptum Dei, caelestem vero amor Dei usque ad contemptum sui.*"

27. Despite the fact that in the Middle Ages the two cities of Augustine were often identified with the institutions of the church and the state, that is not what Augustine is proposing in the *De Civitate Dei*. Later readers of Augustine can be excused, though, as Augustine himself is unclear in his language and often mixes up the categories and expresses differing assessments of the overlap between the spiritual cities and the institutions of society throughout the *De Civitate Dei*. In the Medieval interpretation of the *De*

In books 15-18 Augustine further recounts the development of the two cities. The two cities are predestined to either reign with God or suffer eternal punishment. But first they have to run their course in history, initiated by the fall of Adam. In these books, Augustine is mainly concerned with how the story of the two cities plays out in the biblical stories, but he also relates the course of the two cites to the history of the world. Only in the following books does it become clear how his theory of the two cities in itself entails a new interpretation of the Constantinian shift.

In books 19-22, the last part of the *De Civitate Dei*, Augustine writes about the ends of the two cities. He does this by first offering a critique of the teleological views of ancient philosophy and then explaining his understanding of the last judgment and the final separation of the two cities. It is here, in book 19, that Augustine most cogently lays out his theory of the two cities, and comes the closest to actually expounding his political views.[28] But these last books of the *De Civitate Dei* have to be read on their own terms. Augustine is not offering a discussion on the relations between church and state. Rather, Augustine offers an account of how Christians can live in the empire. Book 19 is preoccupied with definitions of the state and accounts of justice, and not with the details of constitutional practice. That Augustine is not directly discussing the relationship between church and state in book 19, does not mean that the book cannot be used to analyze his interpretation of the Constantinian shift. It is in this book that Augustine's theory of the two cities, the overarching theory that counters Eusebius's interpretation of the Constantinian shift, comes to expression most visibly. After drawing up this short outline of the *De Civitate Dei* it is now possible to turn to an analysis of parts of book 19.

3.3.1 Book 19

Already in book 5, Augustine mentions Constantine by name. Here Augustine explains that Constantine's success is not to be attributed to the fact that he was a Christian. As evidence for such a view, Augustine points to how God removed the Christian emperor Jovian from the throne much

---

Civitate Dei focus was on how Augustine expressed the natural order of society, whereas modern interpretation, rightly, has stressed the eschatological character of Augustine's understanding of the nature of the two cities; see Holsclaw, "Transcending Subjects."

28. O'Daly, *Augustine's City of God*, 209-10.

faster than he did the "apostate emperor" Julian.[29] In his interpretation of the Constantinian shift Augustine has to take into account a history of rulers after Constantine, and this precluded him from a single-stranded embrace of a Christian emperor. In a world where the Christianization of the Roman Empire had not turned out to be the final solution to all problems, the interpretation of the Constantinian shift would necessarily have to become more nuanced. The theological grandeur of such a nuanced interpretation of the Constantinian shift is what comes to full expression in book 19 of the *De Civitate Dei*. As I will look into first, Augustine's concept of two households is what enables him to counter Eusebius's interpretation of the Constantinian shift. As I will examine second, the theory of the two invisible households has implications for how Christians are to relate to visible institutions like the church and the empire.

3.3.2 Two Households

In book 19 we see fully unfolded the wider theological underpinning sustaining Augustine's interpretation of the Constantinian shift. Augustine begins chapter 17 of book 19 by describing two distinct "household of men."[30] One "household of men who do not live by faith strives to find an earthly peace in the goods and advantages which belong to this temporal life,"[31] whereas the other household of men lives by faith and "looks forward to the blessings which are promised as eternal in the life to come."[32] This concept of two communities among human beings provides the framework that enables Augustine to offer a more nuanced interpretation of the Constantinian shift.[33] To have available not only the institutions of the empire

---

29. *ciu.* V:25.

30. *ciu.* XIX:17: "*domus hominum.*" Bettenson translates "household of human beings."

31. *ciu.* XIX:17: "*domus hominum, qui non vivunt ex fide, pacem terrenam ex huius temporalis vitae rebus commodisque sectatur.*"

32. *ciu.* XIX:17: "*domus . . . hominum ex fide viventium expextat ea, quae in futurum aeterna promissa sunt.*"

33. The expression *corpus permixtum* is in the Protestant Church sometimes used as referring to the individual person; at the same time being sinful and sanctified. That might well express the true state of the human condition, and this way of thinking falls in line with Luther's dialectic according to which a human being can be *simul justus et peccator*. But this is not how Augustine used the concept *corpus permixtum*. Augustine used this idea to denote how different people belong to either the one or the other of these two cities. British medieval historian Robert Markus understands it this way: "Membership

and the church, but also two invisible "households of men," penetrating these institutions, offers Augustine more argumentative possibilities. Such new categories makes it possible for Augustine to argue that the institution of the church is not necessarily congruent with the "true" invisible church, and the institutional church's political expressions thereby become less important. The strength of Augustine's ingenious way of interpreting the Constantinian shift is not that he provides a different evaluation of the Constantinian shift but rather that he reevaluates the importance of the question itself.

Does this mean that the people of the household living by faith do not need any of the earthly goods? Do they, for example, not need the protection of the state? Augustine points out that not to be the case. The household of the people living by faith are like pilgrims. They are not captivated by the earthly and temporal things, but instead use them and are sustained by them in their effort to achieve their spiritual goals. According to Augustine, this is also how they relate to political structures and the empire, though these structures have come into existence based on principles not controlled by a Christian desire. Augustine describes how "the earthly city, which does not live by faith, desires an earthly peace and it establishes an ordered concord of civic obedience and rule in order to secure a kind of co-operation of men's wills for the sake of attaining the things which belong to this mortal life."[34] This order they do not strive for based on the virtue of peacefulness in itself, but rather seek due to the fact that it makes society work. Yet "the Heavenly City—or, rather, that part of it which is a pilgrim in this condition of mortality, and which lives by faith—must of necessity make use of this peace also, until this mortal state, for which such peace is necessary, shall have passed away . . . it does not hesitate to obey the laws of the earthly city, whereby the things necessary for the support of this mortal life is administered."[35]

---

of the two cities is mutually exclusive, and there can be no possible overlap; but membership of either is compatible both with belonging to the Roman—or some other—state and with belonging to the Church." See Markus, *Saeculum*, 60–61.

34. ciu. XIX:17: "*terrena civitas, quae non vivit ex fide, terrenam pacem appetit in eoque defigit imperandi oboediendique concordiam civium, ut sit eis de rebus ad mortalem vitam pertinentibus humanarum quaedam compositio voluntatum.*"

35. ciu. XIX:17: "*Civitatis . . . caelestis vel potius pars eius, quae in hac mortalitate peregrinator et vivit ex fide, etiam ista pace necesse est utatur, donec ipsa, cui talis pax necessaria est, mortalitas transeat . . . legibus terrenae civitatis, quibus haec administrantur, quae sustentandae mortali vitae adcommodata sunt, obtemperare non dubitat.*"

Augustine makes it clear that "while the two cities are intermingled, we also make use of the peace of Babylon."[36] Augustine thereby makes creative use of the imagery of the Babylonian captivity. He points out that when the prophet Jeremiah foretold the captivity of the Israelites, he also ordered the captives to pray for the welfare of Babylon.[37] This Old Testament story Augustine connects to the admonition found in the New Testament to pray for kings and people in authority.[38] Augustine is thereby communicating a nuanced message: He is on the one hand pointing out that the empire is not to be opposed or ignored by Christians; they are even to further its thriving. But he is on the other hand saying that the empire is not divine; it is only a temporary arrangement pertaining to Christians in their order of mortality. Hence, the empire is for Augustine something that is to be reckoned with but is not to be ascribed divine authority.

3.3.3 *The Concept of Two Households and Loyalty toward the Empire*

When the empire is relegated to this non-divine position, it becomes possible for Augustine to appeal to a theological authority above the empire. This stands in a stark contrast to Eusebius's interpretation of the Constantinian shift. Eusebius did not appeal to any higher authority than the empire, as he understood the will of the emperor and God to be aligned. Augustine, on the other hand, is limiting the loyalty toward the empire by replacing it with an absolute loyalty toward God:

> Therefore, for as long as this Heavenly City is a pilgrim on earth, she summons [*evoco*][39] citizens of all nations and every tongue,

---

36. *ciu.* XIX:26: "*quamdiu permixtae sunt ambae civitates, utimur et nos pace Babylonis.*"

37. "But seek the welfare of the city where I have sent you into exile, and pray to the Lord on its behalf, for in its welfare you will find your welfare." Jer 29:7 NRSV.

38. "First of all, then, I urge that supplications, prayers, intercessions, and thanksgivings be made for everyone, for kings and all who are in high positions, so that we may lead a quiet and peaceable life in all godliness and dignity." 1 Tim 2:1–2 NRSV.

39. Bettenson translates *ex omnibus gentibus* (gen.pl.) *cives* (acc.pl) *evocat* (3rdps. pres.ind.act.) with "she calls out citizens from all nations." The word *summon*, which Dyson uses, suggests that the Christians are just summoned together, whereas "call out" suggests a more radical break from the temporal world. Such a nuance in translation is worth taking note of, as it influences the interpretation of the relationship between the Church and the rest of creation. According to Lewis and Short, *Latin Dictionary*, both

and brings together a society of pilgrims [peregrinus][40] in which no attention is paid to any differences in the customs, laws, and institutions by which earthly peace is achieved or maintained. She does not rescind or destroy these things, however. For whatever differences there are among the various nations, these all tend towards the same end of earthly peace. Thus, she preserves and follows them, provided only that they do not impede the religion by which we are taught that the one supreme and true God is to be worshipped. And so even the Heavenly City makes use of earthly peace during her pilgrimage, and desires and maintains the cooperation of men's wills in attaining those things which belong to the mortal nature of man, in so far as this may be allowed without prejudice to true godliness and religion.[41]

For Eusebius the empire had a religious significance, and was part of God's plan. As it is seen from the quotation above Augustine instead instills a hierarchy, where the loyalty toward God is to be higher than toward the empire. With that ensured, Augustine is able to admit to Christians the obedience of the laws of the empire while at the same time allow Christians to break the laws of the empire in cases where the loyalty toward God dictates such behavior. But Augustine never explores in detail when it becomes necessary for the Christian to disobey the laws and customs of the state.

It is important to point out that Augustine did believe that God is active within all that happens in history but he is simultaneously maintaining

---

translations fall within the semantic range of *evoco*.

40. Bettenson translates *peregrinus* with "alien" instead of "pilgrim." A society of aliens conveys a different meaning than a society of pilgrims. According to Lewis and Short, *Latin Dictionary*, the term "alien" comes closer to the original meaning of the word, but *peregrinus* later came to be used for a pilgrim. The word alien suggests a more radical difference to the surrounding society, and the choice of word thus affects how the interpretation of the Constantinian shift is perceived by the reader of the English translation of Augustine. It is worth noting how Stanley Hauerwas, who is deeply influenced by John Howard Yoder, titled one of his most widely read books *Resident Aliens: Life in the Christian Colony* (cowritten with William H. Willimon).

41. ciu. XIX:17: "*Haec ergo caelestis civitas dum peregrinatur in terra, ex omnibus gentibus cives evocat atque in omnibus linguis peregrinam colligit societatem, non curans quidquid in moribus legibus institutisque diversum est, quibus pax terrena vel conquiritur vel tenetur, nihil eorum rescindens vel destruens, immo etiam servans ac sequens, quod licet diversum in diversis nationibus, ad unum tamen eundemque finem terrenae pacis intenditur, si religionem, qua unus summus et verus Deus colendus docetur, non impedit. Utitur ergo etiam caelestis civitas in hac sua peregrinatione pace terrena et de rebus ad mortalem hominum naturam pertinentibus humanarum voluntatum compositionem, quantum salva pietate ac religion conceditur.*"

that it is not for humans to identify God's activity. According to Augustine, God worked mysteriously through the political events of history.[42] The distinctive difference between Augustine's and Eusebius's interpretation of the Constantinian shift is thereby not that Eusebius argues that God was active in the Constantinian shift, whereas Augustine argues that God was not active. Characteristic for Augustine's interpretation of the Constantinian shift is instead his persistence that it is not for human beings to identify God's actions in the course of history.[43] The Constantinian shift is from Augustine's point of view of lesser significance as it is not a historical event in which human beings can gauge what is God's will.

The Constantinian shift is for Augustine just a ripple on the surface of God's grander plan for creation. Such an interpretation of the Constantinian shift had consequences for a number of other areas. One of these is the question of war.

3.3.4 The Constantinian Shift and the Theory of Just War

Augustine lived in a time where for more than a century the church had a close connection with the empire. What I want to look into here is how Augustine's interpretation of the Constantinian shift is related to his thinking about war.

The theory of just war (*bellum iustum*) has by many theologians come to be associated with the writings of Augustine of Hippo.[44] The question of when to wage war and whether such a thing as a just war did exist had been dealt with extensively by ancient philosophers, with Cicero's thought laying the foundation for these reflections.[45] But the Constantinian shift made it necessary also for the church to think about this matter, as the church was now entangled in the political actions of the empire. Early theologians like Origen and Tertullian had in passing given thought to this before, but

---

42. Markus, *Saeculum*, 14.

43. Robert Markus sums up this view on history in the following elegant phrase: "Every moment may have its unique and mysterious significance in the ultimate divine *tableau* of men's doings and sufferings; but it is a significance to which God's revelation does not supply the clues." See Markus, *Saeculum*, 21.

44. Mattox, *St. Augustine and the Theory of Just War*, 65. The question of just war as such is not the theme of this book. For a survey of just war theory in Augustine's writings, see Langan, "Elements of St. Augustine's Just War Theory."

45. For an overview of just war theory in ancient philosophy, and an overview of Cicero's influence on these, see Mantovani, *Bellum Iustum*.

now it became necessary for Augustine to recast the question of just war in distinct Christian categories.

As we saw, Augustine was not making a judgment as to whether the Constantinian shift was either good or bad, and his thinking on war takes a similar pattern. According to Augustine, Christians ought essentially to be what we today would term pacifists. However, to live in a fallen world could require participating in war in order to defend the common good, while Augustine still held that war was not mandated by God.[46] For Augustine the Constantinian shift did not mean that the will of God was now being carried out by the empire. Augustine's interpretation of the Constantinian shift allowed him to hold a more nuanced approach to the question of war and the violence exercised by the empire. In chapter 7 of book 19 of the *De Civitate Dei* Augustine described how the fact that people speak different languages is the cause of much trouble and animosity among human beings. That the Roman Empire had forced a common language to be used in the occupied lands had solved some problems "but how many great wars, what slaughter of men, what outpourings of human blood have been necessary to bring this about!"[47] Augustine interprets the Constantinian shift not to mean that the empire was now carrying out the will of God but rather understood it as an occurrence which only changed the surface of the political landscape, but not the underlying nature of the two cities. Therefore Augustine could at the same time allow and be critical toward the violence exerted also by the "Christian" empire, since, according to his interpretation, the empire as such was not doing God's will.[48]

Though Augustine was critical toward violence carried out by the Roman Empire, he claimed that the church sometimes would need to exert violence in order to discipline heretics. Though this would always have to

---

46. Mattox, *St. Augustine and the Theory of Just War*, 85. Augustine did not list criteria for what constituted a just war in the same systematic way as Thomas Aquinas (1225–1274), and subsequently the School of Salamanca, came to do later on.

47. ciu. XIX:7: "sed hoc quam multis et quam grandibus bellis, quanta strage hominum, quanta effusione humani sanguinis comparatum est?"

48. The question of violence exerted by the empire came to be re-interpreted in later protestant, especially Lutheran, theology as the two cities came to be understood as two reigns, both of which God were in control. This departs from Augustine's model, since Augustine's primary metaphor for the church's relation to the world was not citizenship but rather captivity. See Lee, "Republics and Their Loves," 574. Such a later reading of Augustine uses what was for Augustine a critique of the church's embrace of the Constantinian shift to do the opposite and promote Christian obedience to the civil authorities in a manner different to what was intended by Augustine in the *De Civitate Dei*.

be done as a last remedy and with a pastoral aim.[49] For Augustine violence was not in itself a problem, neither when carried out by the state or the church. Such an attitude, according to which the body can be harmed in order to save the internal, the soul, seems to be in congruence with Augustine's emphasis on the internal "invisible" aspects of Christianity. Just war could be waged because ultimately it only pertained to the temporal and did not pertain to the true invisible nature of the church.[50]

3.3.5 Conclusion

If it is true that the *De Civitate Dei* is the autobiography of the Catholic Church, as Thomas Merton suggested, then the writings of Joseph Ratzinger (later Benedict XVI) may be a good help to gain an understanding of the nature of the *De Civitate Dei*. In 1954 Ratzinger published a study (written in 1951) with the title *Volk und Haus Gottes in Augustins Lehre von der Kirche*.[51] Ratzinger states: "Ganz im Gegensatz zum Staatskirchlichen Ansatz . . . hat also Augustin den Stand der Katakombenkirche praktisch zugrundegelegt, als er seine Bestimmung des Verhältnisses von Kirche und Staat entwarf."[52] A church seeking refuge in the catacombs is an image far removed from how Eusebius interpreted the Constantinian shift. I believe Ratzinger has chosen his words wisely, in that they sum up how Augustine was not a proponent of a persecuted church per se, though he was still open for that to be a possibility for the church. Ratzinger saw how for Augustine the Constantinian shift did not mean that the church was either entwined with the Roman Empire or hostile toward the empire; the outlook of society determines the relationship.

Augustine did not have an elaborate historical account of the Constantinian shift in quite the same way as Eusebius did. Instead he countered Eusebius's interpretation of the Constantinian shift with a whole different theological interpretation of history. Augustine's model operates with a

---

49. Markus, *Saeculum*, 140.

50. The question of pacifism and the church becomes vital for Yoder's interpretation of the Constantinian shift, as will become evident in part 4. As a critical remark on Augustine, for now it will suffice to point out how the esteemed New Testament scholar Richard B. Hays has established that "nowhere in the New Testament is there an instance of any writer appealing to a principle such as love or justice to justify actions of violence." See Hays, *Moral Vision of the New Testament*, 339.

51. Ratzinger, *Volk und Haus Gottes in Augustins Lehre von der Kirche*.

52. Ratzinger, *Volk und Haus Gottes in Augustins Lehre von der Kirche*, 316.

distinction between the visible and the invisible church, and thereby manages to disentangle the political occurrences of history from what is God's plan for the world. For Augustine, a hierarchy of loyalty exists, where the loyalty toward God ranks over the loyalty toward the emperor, and Augustine does not allow these to conflate. In such a model this loyalty can lead to the church living in the catacombs or possibly to the church being given an influential voice in society, depending on the context in which the church finds itself.

As Eusebius's interpretation of the Constantinian shift was summed up in five points, I will use similar categories here: (a) Augustine was no sycophant who was attempting to present an interpretation of the Constantinian shift, with the goal of appeasing a secular ruler. Augustine had a thorough theological vision for his interpretation of the Constantinian shift. (b) This theological vision entailed how the interests of the secular ruler and the interests of God could align or they could be contrary to each other. (c) According to Augustine the Constantinian shift was a political occurrence and did not establish the beginning of a new period in history. (d) Augustine did not believe that God's action in history could be easily identified and would therefore not do so when it came to the Constantinian shift. Augustine's theological understanding of the Constantinian shift was rather a corrective as to how to interpret history theologically. (e) Even though Augustine did not perceive of the institutional church as completely identical to the invisible church, he also did not completely separate the institutional church from the invisible church. The Constantinian shift is for Augustine pertaining to the institutional church, but it is not evidence that it will necessarily go Christians well in this world, as the visible institutional church is not the locus for the eschatological realization.

Augustine's interpretation of the Constantinian shift was determined by his theological thinking. Even though he did not agree with Eusebius, they did agree to the extent of having a theological framework for how to think about the question of the relationship between the church and the empire. However, the all-encompassing theopolitical character of Augustine's account of how the church is to be in the world has been forgotten in theological scholarship for a while.

3.4 The Contemporary Debate

For the past two decades an interesting debate has taken place within theological scholarship on the political aspects of Augustine's thought. This debate concerns how Augustine assesses the "secular." On the one side it has been argued that Augustine operates with a neutral *saeculum* where divergent political and religious views can enter into argument (surprisingly like the modern liberal state). On the other side it has been argued that Augustine has a different assessment of the "secular," which does not so readily fit a modern conception of the state. In order to understand Augustine's interpretation of the Constantinian shift, this debate is highly relevant, as it points to questions of how to theologically conceptualize the space which is not the church. How "secular" institutions of society are accounted for influences the interpretation of the Constantinian shift, since the theological evaluation of what is not the church is determinative for how the church's relationship to it is perceived.

Robert Markus's *Saeculum: History and Society in the Theology of St. Augustine* has been highly influential for the understanding of Augustine's political theology.[53] Despite all its qualities, the debate referred to has taken the form of criticizing the view laid out in this book. I will first look at Markus's argument regarding the secular in Augustine's thought and then look into the criticism of it.

3.4.1 Robert Markus's Concept of the Secular

Saeculum: History and Society in the Theology of St. Augustine has for a generation set the standard in the explanation of Augustine's political theory, by which other works would have to be judged.[54] One overarching theory of how Augustine understands the secular governs Markus's interpretation of Augustine's political theory. Markus's interpretation dictates that theologians before Augustine understood the church's relationship to the Roman Empire in one of two ways: either as overly connected to the Empire (as seen in the writings of Eusebius) or as overly hostile to the Empire (as seen

---

53. Markus, *Saeculum*. The book has been published in multiple editions, but without any substantial changes in content. Rowan Williams has referred to the book as "probably the finest survey of Augustine's political thinking in English." See Williams, "Politics and the Soul," 734.

54. O'Donovan, "Political Thought of City of God 19," 48.

in apocalyptic writings).[55] According to Markus, Augustine did not follow any of these views and instead suggested an interpretation which stood in a tension to both these models. Markus presents this as a third way, according to which the Roman Empire is "theologically neutral."[56] Following this interpretation, Markus understands Augustine to argue that since the citizens of the two households are living together in the temporal existence then the space they share, the *res publica,* is a space valued by both, since it is used by the inhabitants of both households to achieve their different goals. By the citizens of the earthly city the relative peace that comes with ordered society is utilized to further pursue their sinful desires, and by the citizens of the heavenly city an ordered society provides a shelter during their pilgrimage in the temporal existence. In Markus's reading of Augustine, the "secular" *res publica* thus gains a positive value.

Markus terms this a positive interpretation of the *res publica* and argues that Augustine imagines the *res publica* as an inherently "pluralistic" place "in which the concerns of individuals with divergent ultimate loyalties coincide."[57] Markus thereby depicts Augustine's vision of the *res publica* as a place that is both pluralistic and theologically neutral. According to Markus, a consequence of Augustine's theory of the two cities is that a third locus is created: a religiously neutral *seaculum*. Markus's interpretation of Augustine thereby lays out a model of society that comes very close to a description of the modern secularized state.

Such a likeness could make one wonder as to whether Markus may be reading Augustine anachronistically in order to utilize him to legitimize the modern secularized state.

3.4.2 Oliver O'Donovan's Critique

In the past couple of decades what is often referred to as "political theology" has had a renaissance within Anglo-Saxon theology. The Radical Orthodoxy movement stands squarely in the center of this revitalization. For Radical Orthodoxy's attempt to regain a distinct theological methodology Augustine plays a pivotal role, and yet John Milbank, one of Radical Orthodoxy's foremost proponents, does not agree with Markus's reading of

---

55. Markus categorizes Cyprian, Tertullian, and the early martyrs as apocalyptic writers. See Markus, *Saeculum*, 55.

56. Markus, *Saeculum*, 55.

57. Markus, *Saeculum*, 69.

Augustine. Milbank points out that Markus makes too strong of a distinction between the visible church and the "city of God on pilgrimage through this world."[58] According to Milbank, such a disconnect works to keep the church invisible and thereby politically impotent.

Milbank formulates a strong criticism of not only Markus's reading of Augustine, but of all forms of the liberal society Markus's interpretation of Augustine supports. Milbank's attempt to recover a pre-enlightenment understanding of theology and the church is impressive but has received strong criticism. British theologian Aidan Nichols has for example pointed out that it comes close to advocating a form of theocracy.[59] As a critique of Milbank's understanding of the relationship between church and state, Stanley Hauerwas famously quipped that Milbank wants the Christians to take over the world, whereas he, more modestly, just wants the church to survive.

A more subtle critique of Markus has been raised by Oliver O'Donovan, who is located theologically somewhere between Milbank and Markus. I find his position to be highly nuanced and a better starting place for a fruitful critique of Markus. O'Donovan is critical toward the liberal state, but instead of propagating a form of theocracy to counter it, he is investigating how the church at the same time can be critical and actively engaged in societies as they are structured in contemporary late capitalism. This goes back to his reading of Augustine.

O'Donovan has pointed out that Markus's reading is anachronistic, since for Augustine an impartial "naked public square" does not exist and for Augustine a commonweal can only be just where God is honored through right worship.[60] O'Donovan argues that for Augustine there is no *tertium quid* between the two households. There is no such thing as a neutral space in which the members of the two households meet as equal partners. O'Donovan points out how Markus multiple times reaches for the word "state" to explain Augustine's idea of a *saeculum* but O'Donovan argues that Augustine "had no conception of 'state.'"[61] Rome is not a "state" but rather a *civitas*: a concrete body of people. The only thing common

---

58. Milbank, *Theology and Social Theory*, 406.
59. Nichols, "Non tali auxilio."
60. O'Donovan, "Political Thought of City of God 19," 55.
61. O'Donovan, "Political Thought of City of God 19," 59.

to citizens of both the heavenly and the earthly city is a shared desire for peace. They did not share an institution but rather a condition of order.[62]

O'Donovan points out that in Markus's interpretation, one can be a member of either the heavenly or the earthly city and still be a member of the Roman Empire.[63] But O'Donovan suggests that this goes beyond Augustine "for whom, it would seem, true Christians were never true Romans (in the sense of being part of the Roman imperial project) nor false Christians true members of the church (in the sense of being part of the pilgrim society)."[64] According to O'Donovan there is in the *De Civitate Dei* no value-free *tertium quid* that could serve as a neutral secular space. I find that to be an astute critique of Robert Markus's interpretation of Augustine; a critique that essentially points out that Markus is guilty in an anachronistic reading of Augustine that reads Enlightenment ideas about secular society into Augustine.[65] How did Markus react to this critique?

In Markus's response to this critique we encounter an example of the very Augustinian, but seldom seen, academic virtue of reexamining, retracting and conceding defeat to the better argument. In his 2006 book *Christianity and the Secular* Robert Markus describes how the climate of 1970 wherein he wrote *Saeculum: History and Society in the Theology of St. Augustine* was influenced by theories of an imminent secularization.[66] This influence, Markus admits, informed his interpretation of Augustine. He was led to see Augustine as one of the founding fathers of Western secularity.[67] The third chapter of his book Markus dedicates to both acknowledging where he went wrong regarding Augustine's understanding of the secular, and defending the idea that Augustine does ascribe positive value to the

---

62. O'Donovan, "Political Thought of City of God 19," 59.

63. See Markus, *Saeculum*, 60–62.

64. O'Donovan, "Political Thought of City of God 19," 59.

65. Markus cannot be accused of concealing that he took his contemporary political situation into account in his reading of Augustine in 1970: "To go back to Augustine merely with a view to finding in his work warrant for some particular theological position would be suspect; certainly suspect as historical scholarship, but also suspect as sound theology. But to return to Augustine and to 'carve a channel' from him to our own times, to find oneself, willing or unwilling, involved in a dialogue with him on questions agitating theology today, cannot be condemned as unsound, either in historical or in theological procedure." See Markus, *Saeculum*, ix.

66. Markus, *Christianity and the Secular*.

67. Markus, *Christianity and the Secular*, 3.

state.⁶⁸ Thus, both O'Donovan and Markus agree that Markus's reading of Augustine in his 1970 book had flaws.

I will not pursue this debate between Markus and O'Donovan any further here. But how is all this relevant for an analysis of Augustine's interpretation of the Constantinian shift? It can be concluded that Augustine's assessment of the secular does not work to support the modern liberal state. According to this revised understanding of Augustine, he was not an early agitator for the formation of a neutral secular state.⁶⁹ Augustine was thereby not only critical toward the way Eusebius interpreted the Constantinian shift, but would presumably also turn against how the relationship between church and state has come to be understood and tacitly supported by most churches in the Western world since the Enlightenment.

On the second to last page of his book *Christianity and the Secular* Markus suggests that "what some theologians have called 'Constantinianism' is, at bottom, obliviousness to the crucial gap between the Church and the world, and 'Christendom' is the name under which the state of affairs corresponding to it has generally come to be designated."⁷⁰ It seems like Robert Markus, in the end, does interpret Augustine in a way that comes close to the critical view of the Constantinian shift, which Yoder would raise more than 1,500 years after the completion of the *De Civitate Dei*.⁷¹

Though, before moving on to Yoder, I first want to look into what separates Eusebius's and Augustine's interpretations of the Constantinian shift. This will serve as a good preparation for the final comparison of the three interpretations of the Constantinian shift in the end of part 4.

---

68. In good Augustinian style, Markus himself refers to this as a *retractatio*. See Markus, *Christianity and the Secular*, 51. In line with Augustine's use of this genre, Markus at the same time retracts and defends earlier held views.

69. William Cavanaugh stresses this point by arguing how the existence of a secular coercive government for Augustine is nothing but a tragic reality, and he points out that Augustine in the *De Civitate Dei* is not giving us "anything like a theory of church and state, or civil society and state. There is no division of sacred and secular, private and public, no division of labour between the things that are Caesar's and the things that are God's for, as Dorothy Day once commented, if you give to God what is God's, there is nothing left for Caesar." See Cavanaugh, "From One City to Two," 312.

70. Markus, *Christianity and the Secular*, 90.

71. Though Markus does also in 2006 criticize Yoder for not ascribing enough positive value to the secular realm. See Markus, *Christianity and the Secular*, 25–26.

3.5 Augustine and Eusebius (Interior Differences)

Multiple dissimilarities could be pointed out between how Eusebius and Augustine arrived at their interpretations of the Constantinian shift, but here I will concentrate on what are the three main differences pertinent to the emergence of Eusebius's and Augustine's interpretation of the Constantinian shift. These are: differences in their theological sources, differences in their understanding of history, and differences in their theological method. They did share, though, the view on the theological nature of a historical account. After looking into these variances, it is possible to arrive at a preliminary comparison between their interpretations of the Constantinian shift.

3.5.1 Different Theological Sources

Augustine and Eusebius drew their theological inspiration from disparate sources; it could be claimed that when comparing the interpretation of the Constantinian shift as expressed in the *Vita Constantini* and in the *De Civitate Dei,* one is actually engaging a comparison between Eastern and Western theology. As we saw spelled out in part 2 Eusebius was influenced by Origen. Augustine, on the other hand, was critical of the tendentiously Pelagian ideas of sanctification of which Origen could be seen as a forbearer.[72] Augustine held that the influence of sin was pervasive, and Augustine's teaching on original sin took a very different form than that of Origen.[73] This foundational dissimilarity plays a role in the way Eusebius and Augustine differ in their interpretation of the Constantinian shift. Eusebius understands the Constantinian shift as a progression of human affairs; an

---

72. In 415, while writing the *De Civitate Dei*, Augustine authored the treatise *Contra Priscillianistas et Origenistas*, where he attacked Origenist theology. Also in the *De Civitate Dei*, Augustine offers at critique of Origen's idea that the devil and his angels will eventually be freed from punishment and united with the holy angels. See *ciu.* XXI:17. However, Augustine was at the same time influenced to some extent by Origen's theology, especially in his exegetical work. Augustine was probably cautious to state this publicly due to the danger of being too closely associated with Origen after the Origenist controversies in the late fourth century. See Bammel, "Augustine, Origen and the Exegesis of St. Paul."

73. For a succinct account of Augustine's teaching on original sin, see Couenhoven, "St. Augustine's Doctrine of Original Sin." Couenhoven points out that Augustine does not have a singular teaching on original sin. He instead identifies five elements, which, albeit in a continual tension, come to form what later has been conceived as one unified doctrine.

interpretation supported by a theological presupposition that not only can an individual person improve him or herself, but a whole empire can improve and can be carrying out God's plan. Augustine's stronger awareness of the influence of sin prevented him from such a high view on the potential improvement of any human affair.[74]

According to Augustine the Christianization of the empire is a matter of less interest. O'Daly points out that Augustine does not see the conversion of Constantine as a "watershed" but considers the Roman Empire to basically remain the same after that event.[75] That has to do with Augustine's conception of the Christian faith: Augustine stands as one of the prime thinkers among the Western theologians who are starting a process of internalization of Christianity.[76] That the Christianization of the emperor and the Roman Empire is not ascribed special importance by Augustine is a consequence of Augustine's way of understanding Christian faith. Whereas Eusebius was inspired by what was later to be identified as Eastern theology, and upholds the possibility of identifying the progress of society with the Constantinian shift, Augustine is working in an emerging Western theological tradition, which emphasizes an internal relationship with God.[77] According to such a theological approach, God's providence expressed itself rather in the concealed drama of sin and redemption than in grand political events.[78]

Augustine writes in book five of the *De Civitate Dei*: "As far as this mortal life is concerned, which is spent and finished in a few days, what difference does it make under what rule a man lives who is soon to die, provided only that those who rule him do not compel him to do what is

74. How the traditionally Eastern Orthodox theological concept of divinization influences Eusebius's interpretation of the Constantinian shift, I will return to in part 4.

75. O'Daly, *Augustine's City of God*, 205.

76. Augustine, *Augustine of Hippo*, xi–58. Augustine was by no means the sole initiator of the internalistic and individualistic direction that Western theology and philosophy later came to take. See Dumont, *Essays on Individualism*, 23–59. Little doubt is left, though, that with the *Confessiones* and his way of internalizing Christian belief Augustine did break a new path; even from the sources that he was most inspired by. As E. R. Dodds put it: "Plotinus never gossiped with the One as Augustine gossiped in the *Confessions*" (quotation found in Augustine, *Augustine of Hippo*, xiii—though the last name of Eric Robertson Dodds (1893–1979) is misspelled as Dodd; possibly due to a confusion in names with Marcus Dods (1834–1909), the translator of Augustine).

77. For an overview of Augustine's sources of inspiration and what led Augustine to form his theological views, see the chapter "Influences and Sources" in O'Daly, *Augustine's City of God*, 234–64.

78. Chesnut, "Pattern of the Past," 81.

impious and wicked?"[79] It is clear that Augustine is writing after the Constantinian shift where it was not common that the emperor forced Christians to worship Roman gods etc. When everyone are Christian the outer and visible aspects of Christianity were no longer distinctive, and the core of Christianity logically moved inside the individual and became invisible. The Constantinian shift in that way in itself showed the way to the internalization of Christianity.

Augustine skillfully utilizes this internalization of Christianity to reinterpret the Constantinian shift and assign less significance to the "institutional" visible church.[80] In his influential essay "The Apostle Paul and the Introspective Conscience of the West" Krister Stendahl argues that Augustine "may well have been one of the first to express the dilemma of the introspective conscience."[81] According to Stendahl this was a new conception in the early church, which led to both a different evaluation of the church and a way of reading Paul different from how he had been read by early Christians.[82] Such an internalization of the Christian life was bound to drive Augustine to an interpretation of the Constantinian shift that differed from Eusebius's interpretation, due to the fact that Eusebius was inspired by the ideas of a visible process of divinization. However, Augustine interpreted the Constantinian shift based on a theology on internalization,

---

79. *ciu.* V:17: "*Quantum enim pertinet ad hanc vitam mortalium, quae paucis diebus ducitur et finitur, quid interest sub cuius imperio vivat homo moriturus, si illi qui imperant ad impia et iniqua non cogant?*"

80. An interesting structural similarity is to be found between the later Eastern emphasis on the importance of the outer visible form of the church and the importance that a theologically Western movement like the Anabaptist churches came to ascribe to the witness given by the outer form of the church. In part 4 I will look into how both Eusebius and a Mennonite theologian like John Howard Yoder can ascribe such importance to the outer form of the church, but at the same time interpret the Constantinian shift radically different.

81. Stendahl, "Apostle Paul and the Introspective Conscience of the West," 203.

82. Stendahl argues that Luther takes Augustine's internal view of faith even further, and instead of understanding the Jewish Law as pertaining to practical questions of how to live life, it was by Luther, though started by Augustine, transformed into an abstract law that had the function of leading Christians to grace, i.e., Luther's second use of the law; Stendahl, "Apostle Paul," 206. That a connection can be made between this early misunderstanding of the Jewish Law as negative and punitive (when it was actually conceived as a blessing that guarded the covenant between God and human beings), and the sparsely developed theology of sanctification and the visible church within Lutheran theology, I do not hold to be a controversial claim.

which in effect already presupposed a Constantinian shift and an emperor friendly to Christianity.

A different evaluation of the visible institutional church also led Augustine to perceive differently how God's plan for the world was realized throughout history.

3.5.2 *The Purpose of Writing a Historical Account*

It is not all dissimilarities, though. When it comes to the purpose of historical writing Augustine and Eusebius share views. In the *De Civitate Dei* Augustine makes a telling remark on historical writing. He says that if he were to recount the details of how many towns had been destroyed or ships had been sunk during the Punic wars then "I should turn into just another chronicler [*scriptor*]."[83] With this remark, Augustine dissociates himself both from his own disciple Paulus Orosius and the fourth-century Roman historian Ammianus Marcellinus (ca. 330–ca. 395), as Augustine does not want to write a history which recounted the development of a specific historical kingdom or a specific battle.[84] The aim for Augustine is something different: to utilize history in expressing a theological vision and thereby employ history to educate the reader regarding the content of the Christian faith. That is quite different from how the discipline of history is understood today, after the influence from a positivist conception of history and its desire to recount history *wie es eigentlich gewesen*.[85] Likewise, *De Civitate Dei* is at the same time a piece of historical writing and a theological treatise, and in this regard, it does not differ from either the writings of Eusebius of Caesarea or of John Howard Yoder.

---

83. *ciu.* III:18: "*nihil aliud quam scriptores etiam nos erimus historiae.*" Bettenson translates this in the singular, and as an exception I have used his translation.

84. Markus, *Saeculum*, 2.

85. By quoting von Ranke's famous saying from 1824, I am alluding to what this saying has been taken to mean, rather than what Ranke attempted to express. Georg Iggers in 1962 pointed out that Ranke's statement in the hands of positivist nineteenth-century historians had been understood as an appeal to recount the bare facts of what had happened. But the *eigentlich* in Ranke's statement does not refer to just bare facts, but rather to the inner meaning of what had happened; an interpretation much more in line with Ranke's philosophical idealism. See Iggers, "The Image of Ranke in American and German Historical Thought." Ranke's original intention can then serve as a timely reminder not to read Eusebius and Augustine on our terms but to read them in concord with how they understood the writing of history.

The Christian narrative contains a multitude of claims located within a specific time and place in history, and theology has therefore from the outset been dealing with history.[86] But as part of Augustine's interest in using history didactically came also the concern of incorporating the historical events of Christianity into the scope of wider world history. Yet, how the historical account relates to the theological message can be conceived differently. For Augustine it was important to situate the *historia sacra* (the biblical story of the world) within the wider frame of the *historia saecula* (world history). The existence of both a *historia sacra* and a *historia saecula* was not doubted by either Eusebius or Augustine. Both in regard to using history for the goal of Christian education and in wanting to locate the historical events of Christianity within the broader history of the world, Augustine shared views with his episcopal colleague Eusebius.[87] They shared the view that writing history could be a way of expressing a theological view, but they differed as to which events were to be considered part of the *historia sacra* and the *historia saecula*.

What are God's plans and what are the plans of human beings and how to distinguish? Grand questions come up in the following.

3.5.3 Different Conception of the Progression of History

What theological message did Augustine want to convey in his historical account? Was it the same message of progress, which Eusebius expressed in his interpretation of the Constantinian shift? The answer is no. In Augustine's view the time between the incarnation and the *parousia* is a period of unknown duration perceived as a theologically "blank" filled with an infinite variety of occurrences but none theologically privileged above others. Augustine does not imply that God left human beings to their own devices after the incarnation, but he believes the very limited means of our cognition makes it impossible for the human mind to identify how God is active in the history of the world. God's actions in wider history are hidden; only in the biblical revelation an account of them are to be found. Robert Markus thus sums up Augustine's view: "God's hand and God's purposes are equally present and equally hidden in them [events in history] all."[88]

---

86. The crucifixion and resurrection of Jesus Christ is probably the foremost example of the historical specificity of the Christian gospel.

87. Markus, *Saeculum*, 6.

88. Markus, *Saeculum*, 23.

Eusebius, in his view of history, does not operate with the same clear distinction between a *historia sacra* and a *historia saecula* as is found in Augustine. According to Eusebius, the Constantinian shift was an event in which God was active in the world and Eusebius consequently interprets this as part of the sacred history playing out in the wider history of the world. The Constantinian shift does not fall into this category for Augustine. For him the Constantinian shift was just another political occurrence in the jumble of events between the incarnation and the *parousia*, and therefore not part of sacred history. Augustine does believe God is active in history; but for Augustine the Constantinian shift was not an event where God's possible actions could be identified.

It is worth noting that Augustine held millenarian views at an earlier point in his life, which came close to the concept of a *tempora christiana*, according to which the Christianization of the emperors is interpreted as the beginning of a special Christian time in the history of the world.[89] But Augustine moved away from this understanding of history, and had only a wry comment on people who identified the success of the institutional church with Christian triumph: "The very same people who fill the churches on the festivals of Jerusalem fill the theatres for the festivities of Babylon."[90]

Regarding Eusebius's and Augustine's understanding of history, it can be concluded that they agreed regarding the method of writing history in order to express a theological vision, but they disagreed in their views on the progression of the course of history and where to identify the sacred history and the wider history of the world.[91] Their dissimilar views on whether God's intervention in history after the incarnation can or cannot be identified is a key factor for the understanding of their different interpretations

---

89. Markus identifies the period around 414 as the time when Augustine reached his mature views on sacred and profane history. Markus argues that Augustine had here come to see "sacred history" as confined to the history to be found within the scriptural canon, and Augustine denied this status to any other interpretations of historical events in the writings following 414. See Markus, *Saeculum*, 43.

90. "Qui sollemnitatibus Ierusalem implent Ecclesias, sollemnitatibus Babyloniae implent theatra." *Enarrationes in Psalmos* LXI:10. English translation found in Markus, *Saeculum*, 40.

91. Robert Markus has received criticism for arguing that Augustine turned against millenarian points of view. For Markus's rebuttal of this critique, see Markus, "Tempora Christiana Revisited." The debate as to what Augustine's theology of history would look like has been going on in the scholarly literature since at least the 1970s. See O'Daly, *Augustine's City of God*, 194.

of the Constantinian shift. For Eusebius the Constantinian shift was an act of God, whereas Augustine thought it impossible to make such judgment.

3.5.4 Different Theological Framework

Throughout his life Augustine had the intellectual honesty to abandon previously held standpoints. This practice led to Augustine becoming well trained in criticizing systems of thought that he had agreed with earlier but did not any longer.[92] It might be these experiences of criticizing earlier held standpoints, which equipped Augustine with the ability to mount an elaborate critique of Eusebius's interpretation of the Constantinian shift, since Augustine himself earlier had held millenarian views that pointed to an interpretation of the Constantinian shift similar to that of Eusebius. At the time of Augustine Eusebius's interpretation of the Constantinian shift was pervasive. Instead of working in the same framework as Eusebius, Augustine changed the whole outlay of how to interpret the Constantinian shift. It became necessary for Augustine to conceive of a different way of interpreting historical events and the relationship between the church and worldly empires.

Instead of describing the Constantinian shift in minute detail, Augustine expressed his theological interpretation of the Constantinian shift on a larger scale. Since Augustine did not think it possible to identify the actions of God in the details of history, as Eusebius had done, it became necessary for the bishop of Hippo to lay out a grander scheme of God's acts and involvement in the world. From the perspective of this grander scheme, the events in the course of history could then be interpreted theologically. The theology of the "two cities" serves as the framework for this grand scheme. Augustine thereby could counter Eusebius's interpretation of the Constantinian shift; not by giving another interpretation as such, but by changing the understanding of how to interpret history. According to Augustine's view of history and the theory of the two households, a political event like the Constantinian shift was nothing but a ripple on the surface of God's greater plan.

---

92. See for example books 5–8 of *Confessiones* (finished in 398), where Augustine recounts how he moved away from Manichean beliefs.

3.6 Conclusion

Both Eusebius and Augustine had a theological framework for their interpretation of the Constantinian shift. None of them were sycophants who merely appeased political powers, instead they were bishops who had a theological vision for their work. As we saw, this similarity came to expression in the way they conceived of the study of history, in that they believed it ought to express a theological vision and educate the reader theologically. Though they interpreted the Constantinian shift differently, both Eusebius's and Augustine's work is framed by a theological vision for how to imagine the church in the world.

They did differ, though, on how the church was to be in the world. For Augustine, the success of the empire and the church did not align neatly as it did in Eusebius's interpretation. This dissimilarity had to do with their differing views on the progression of history. For Augustine, the Constantinian shift was not understood as an omen for the beginning of a new epoch in history, as he perceived it as any political event between the incarnation and the *parousia*. How God acted in history was according to Augustine not for human beings to judge. Their different attitude to war illustrated that principle. For Eusebius the war of the empire was sanctioned by God and it was less of a moral question. For Augustine a political occurrence like the empire's engagement in war was not sanctioned by God. That made it necessary for Augustine to develop a theory for when a war was just to decide whether engaging in a war was defensible.

Contrary to Eusebius, Augustine did not interpret the Constantinian shift as evidence that it would go Christians well in this world. For Augustine, the spiritual church was not tied up with the institutional church in the same way as it was for Eusebius, and political occurrences could thereby not change the ultimate goal of the church. The question of the ultimate goal of the church and the world can be rephrased as a question of eschatology. The comparison of Eusebius's and Augustine's interpretations of the Constantinian shift revealed two differing eschatological visions. For Eusebius the success of the church in the history of the world reflected God's plan, whereas this was not the case for Augustine, who only in the *eschaton* saw the realization of what the church was to become. The eschatological vision is determinative for how the role of the church in the world is envisioned and thereby gains influence on Eusebius's and Augustine's interpretation of the Constantinian shift. In the next part of this book, I will look into how different eschatological visions help to shape different interpretations of the Constantinian shift.

Contemporary scholarship has pointed out how both Eusebius and Augustine earlier had been read in a way that failed to take into account the encompassing theological scope of their thinking. Despite their different interpretations of the Constantinian shift both Eusebius and Augustine had a theology according to which both the church, the empire, and their relationship were narrated theologically. The thoroughly theological character of their interpretations of the Constantinian shift makes them excellent conversation partners with John Howard Yoder.

Andrew Ward has compared Augustine's context to the contemporary intellectual environment in the West: "Poised as he was on the threshold between radical pluralism (which he called paganism) and the rise of Christendom, we stand on the other side of that history: at the end of Christendom and the reemergence of radical (as distinct from liberal) pluralism."[93] The cultural climate today is different from Augustine's, but, as Ward suggests, at the same time there are structural similarities between the pluralism of the fourth century and the intellectual context of a contemporary globalized West. By the fourth and fifth centuries the church had gradually moved closer to the center of political power. In present time the church in the Western world has for the past centuries moved away from political power. The situation for the church in the West today is, though the direction is the opposite, structurally similar to the situation at the time of Augustine, in that the church has to define its place anew after an alteration in its connection to political powers. This changed situation has called for a new interpretation of the relationship between church and state and a reevaluation of the account of the Constantinian shift. On the coming pages I will investigate how John Howard Yoder's work represents such a paradigmatic contemporary interpretation of the Constantinian shift.

---

93. Ward, "Questioning God," 277.

PART IV:

A Current Interpretation

4
John Howard Yoder

4.1 Introduction

"Christians in the first century were a minority in a hostile world. Their ethical views were attuned to that context. In the twentieth century, Christians . . . are also in a minority in a world committed to other loyalties, yet we do not reason as the Early Christians did."[1] John Howard Yoder asks what has happened, so that the ethic of the church in the Western world is perceived as being aligned with the world instead of the church being a virtuous community standing out from the world? Yoder points to one historical event as the point where the early church began to change from being a peacemaking moral community of character to an accommodationist supporter of the empire: the Constantinian shift. For Yoder the preoccupation with the Constantinian shift is not just an academic endeavor, but the understanding of this historical event is important for him as it plays a key role in making the church regain its right place in the world. Thereby Yoder's strong reinvigoration of earlier Anabaptist ideas about the Constantinian shift made it the most persistent theme in his work.[2] Very much like Eusebius's and Augustine's work, Yoder's interpretation of the Constantinian shift thus is at the same time a work of history and of theology.

In order to commence the analysis of this the third interpretation of the Constantinian shift, I will begin by giving a short account of the life of Yoder. He hailed from a different denominational background than most

1. Yoder, *Priestly Kingdom*, 135.
2. Huebner and Hauerwas, *Precarious Peace*, 57.

contemporary academic theologians, and hence a short biography of his life will help to understand how he came to understand his task as a historian and a theologian. These descriptions will together constitute the first section. In the long second section I will provide an outline of three essays, where Yoder's interpretation of the Constantinian shift most succinctly finds expression. That will enable me to move on to a detailed analysis of Yoder's interpretation of the Constantinian shift and an analysis of the way he utilizes this interpretation to criticize the contemporary church. Based on this analysis of his work I can draw a preliminary conclusion on his interpretation of the Constantinian shift.

Yoder's interpretation of the Constantinian shift has been criticized on both historical and theological grounds in contemporary scholarship. This criticism I will look at in a third section, before moving on to the last section in this part 4; the comparison of Yoder's interpretation of the Constantinian shift with the two ancient interpretations. This forms the final comparison between the three interpretations of the Constantinian shift.

4.1.1 Yoder as Theologian and Historian

John Howard Yoder (1927–1997) was born in an old Mennonite family from Ohio, USA. This came to set the course of his career, as Radical Reformation theology exerted a deep influence on his theology and his understanding of the Constantinian shift.[3] Historically the churches born out of the Radical Reformation have prioritized lived Christian life over theoretical debates on the nature of Christianity. This different interest led to questions of how to live in the world, and the differing view on the secular

3. In his essay "Anabaptists in the Continental Reformation" Yoder examines by what name to refer to the churches, which were products of the so-called left wing of the Reformation. See Yoder, *Christian Attitudes to War, Peace, and Revolution*, 161–95. He argues that given not all of these churches actually believed in re-baptism, the term "Anabaptist" is deficient. Yoder instead ponders whether to use "Free church," "Believers church," or "Historic peace church," only to conclude that "Radical Reformation church" is the most appropriate term, since this term "accentuates the fact that this narrowing process takes place in church history, in times of change and reform. We are interested in the movement toward the center of that circle." See Yoder, *Christian Attitudes to War, Peace, and Revolution*, 162. At other instances, though, Yoder claimed that he preferred the term "Believers Church," since it is a term less strict on which churches belong in that group. He liked such a "fuzzy term," since it is characterized by an unclear boundary, but a clear center. See Yoder, "Historiography as a Ministry to Renewal," 220. Throughout this book Radical Reformation is the preferred term, though "Anabaptism" has been applied where the sources investigated make use of this term.

authority has constituted one of the primary dividing factors between the Magisterial Reformation and the Radical Reformation; thus the question of how to interpret the Constantinian shift naturally came to take a central place for Yoder in order to situate himself in relation to theologians from other protestant traditions.[4] Yoder gave new life to the Radical Reformation interpretation of the Constantinian shift and is almost singularly responsible for putting Mennonite theology on the theological map at the end of the twentieth century.[5]

After his undergraduate studies at Mennonite Goshen College in Indiana, Yoder went to France to work for the Mennonite Church, later enrolling at studies in Basel, Switzerland. Yoder met Anne Marie Guth in France and they married in 1952.[6] However, Yoder later would be guilty of sexual abuse toward a number of women.[7]

---

4. An illustrative (and not completely objective) exposition of how the Radical Reformation tradition interpreted the Reformation is given by William Estep: "The Anabaptist interpretation of the church's fall differed greatly from that of the Reformers. The Reformers apparently accepted uncritically the Roman interpretation of the Constantinian era as a period of the church's triumph. In so doing they fell victim to the Constantinian symbiosis unwittingly embracing a pre-Christian sacral society whose paganism they conveniently overlooked or christened and sought to regulate. For them the Reformation was a revolt against papal authority but not against the Roman concept of the church as an institution. They believed that the old church needed to be cleansed from various abuses and errors, but they did not want to be cut off from its corporate solidarity. Even after their organizational break with Rome was complete, they still felt a sense of continuity with the Roman Church of Pre-reformation days." See Estep, *Anabaptist Story*, 242.

5. Nation, "John Howard Yoder," 357.

6. Nation, "John Howard Yoder," 361.

7. Yoder engaged in intimate relationships with a large number of his female students and was guilty of sexual abuse. An article in the New York Times on Yoder's sexual misconduct opens with the straightforward question "Can a bad person be a good theologian?" See Oppenheimer, "A Theologian's Influence." Not least because Yoder in his theological writings vehemently argued that the personal lives and virtues of theologians cannot be detached from their theology, this matter requires comment. Brad East, who in 2017 finished his dissertation, partly on Yoder's theology of Scripture, suggests that Yoder's sexual misconduct ought to be at least mentioned in any academic treatment of his work. See East, "On Being a Scholar of John Howard Yoder." A number of scholars have recently pointed out how the conversation regarding Yoder's sexual abuse tends to focus on Yoder and not the victims. For a thorough report on Yoder's victims and how the case was handled by the Mennonite Church, see Goosen, "Defanging the Beast," 7–80. For Stanley Haerwas's response, see "In Defence of 'Our Respectable Culture.'" For a critique of Hauerwas's response, see Scarsella, "Not Making Sense," and see Hunter-Bowman, "The Opportunity Stanley Hauerwas Missed."

At Goshen, Yoder had come under influence of the prominent Mennonite historian Harold Bender (1897–1962), who had worked to rehabilitate the story of the Mennonite church, and give it a fair treatment based on the writings of the Radical Reformation churches instead of only relying on the polemical works of their enemies.[8] During the complicated years of World War II, Bender had worked with the history of pacifism in the churches springing from the Radical Reformation, and this came to have a lasting influence on Yoder's scholarship.[9] In addition Yoder's theological schooling in Europe exposed him to teachers as different as Walther Baumgartner (Old Testament), Oscar Cullmann (New Testament), Karl Jaspers (Philosophy) and Karl Barth (Dogmatics).[10]

In 1954, Yoder finished the dissertation *Täufertum und Reformation in der Schweiz: Die Gespräche zwischen Täufern und Reformatoren 1523–1538* in church history.[11] In his dissertation Yoder built on Bender's work, which argued that the first Anabaptists came from followers of Zwingli, leading Bender to conclude that Anabaptism was the culmination of the Reformation: The fulfillment of the original vision of Luther and Zwingli to recreate the original New Testament church.[12] In the first part of his dissertation, Yoder examines predominantly the correspondences of Zwingli in order to prove that he had initially aimed to form an independent "believer's church" but eventually came to accept an alliance with the civil authorities in order to form a state church. In the second part of his dissertation, Yoder examines the theology of these early Anabaptist churches and relates their theology to the situation of persecution in which they had arisen. The dissertation thereby came to be typical for Yoder's later work of uniting the disciplines of history, ethics and dogmatics.[13]

8. Dyck, *Introduction to Mennonite History*, 34.

9. In his 1944 essay "Anabaptist Vision," Bender identifies three main characteristics of the churches springing form the Radical Reformation: "A new conception of the essence of Christianity as discipleship; second, a new conception of the church as a brotherhood; and third, a new ethic of love and nonresistance." See Bender, "Anabaptist Vision," 42. All traits which are to be found in Yoder's theology.

10. Nikolajsen, *Distinctive Identity of the Church*, 96.

11. For the dissertation in German, see Yoder, *Täufertum und Reformation in der Schweiz: Die Gespräche zwischen Täufern und Reformatoren 1523–1538* (1962); for an English translation and an introduction to the dissertation, see Yoder, *Anabaptism and Reformation in Switzerland* (2004).

12. Yoder, *Anabaptism and Reformation in Switzerland*, xvi.

13. In the mid-seventies James Stayer et al. published a renowned article arguing for a theory of "polygenesis" instead of "monogenesis" in regard to the emergence of the

John Howard Yoder

Yoder returned to the US in 1957 and came to work at various theological and ecumenical institutions before he in 1977 eventually took the position of professor of Theology at the University of Notre Dame, which he held until his death in 1997.[14] Yoder came to influence theologians from many different traditions, most prominently Stanley Hauerwas whose writings are to be accredited as the main instigation of the so-called antirealist direction in contemporary theological thinking about politics.[15]

In his theological work, Yoder rejected any form of strict method or system, as he wanted to avoid a tendency toward what he called "methodologism" in theology.[16] Yoder's work did not stick to one method in how to approach theological questions, and he had no guiding systematic principle for his theological writing. With that being said, the question of the Constantinian shift did form a constant in his work, and connects to the other main themes of his work: Christian pacifism, the pointing out of the close connection between the Old Testament and the New Testament, and the ecumenical strands in his writing.[17]

Anabaptist churches. According to Stayer's theory the Anabaptist churches could not be traced back to one origin, but instead have arisen independently at multiple places. See Stayer et al., "From Monogenesis to Polygenesis." This theory was not congruent with Yoder's work, and from the seventies and onwards, direct historical work came to occupy less and less space in Yoder's quickly expanding writings. Yoder was instead occupied with investigating the historical sources from the perspective of theological questions in regard to how a faithful church should be ordered, and how the church should relate to the state, though such questions has increasingly been ruled out by traditional Reformation historians. See Yoder, *Anabaptism and Reformation in Switzerland*, xxix.

14. Nikolajsen, *Distinctive Identity of the Church*, 97.

15. Leithart, *Defending Constantine*, 11. The term "antirealist" here denotes a form of political theology that takes its starting point not in what seems immediately plausible but instead formulates what is found to be a faithful way of following Christ in the current context of the church—hoping this approach in the end will constitute the most responsible course of action for the church. As I will later look into in this chapter, such "antirealism" is countered by a "realist" approach that argues for the church to take political responsibility for the development of society.

16. Nation, *John Howard Yoder*, 137.

17. Yoder thereby inscribes himself among the theologians, who's passionate questions pertaining to the relevance of the concrete life of Jesus Christ prohibits a grand theological system. Stanley Hauerwas puts it this way: "So there is no 'center' to Yoder's thought. Not even nonviolence is a systematic principle for him. Jesus is central, of course, but since Jesus is the Son of God, that means he is the center that cannot be summarized, because Jesus makes a difference for how everything is understood. Yoder's work, therefore, is not 'systematic.'" See Nation, *John Howard Yoder*, xi. Søren Kierkegaard is the paradigmatic example of a theologian who, for similar reasons, eschewed the concept of a system in theology.

Yoder used the concepts of the Constantinian shift and Constantinianism not merely to refer to historical events but also as narrative tropes, as they became a way to name an ecclesiological pitfall in which the church had accommodated itself to the common ethic of society instead of following the example of Christ.[18] One must not overlook this aspect of Yoder's treatment of the Constantinian shift and read his interpretation of the Constantinian shift on purely historical grounds; for he was, in fact, constructing a theology via his interpretation of the Constantinian shift. To avoid such a misreading I will now look into how Yoder conceived of the study of history in relation to theology and politics.

4.1.2 Yoder as a Mennonite Historian

"Reformation is like getting up from a fall; radical reformation like getting back to where one got off the track."[19] In the essay "Historiography as a Ministry of Renewal" Yoder referred to the study of history as the "ministry of remembrance," as he understood the study of history to serve to "trace the sameness of Jesus and his message across the generations."[20] As Yoder was inspired by Radical Reformation theology, which often idealizes not only the theology but also the organization of the early church, it became important for him to investigate the Constantinian shift, as he believed it instilled a profound change in the way the church perceived of its position in the world.

For Yoder the history of Christianity must be read in the light of the deep shift, which took place in the relationship between the church and the world with the Constantinian shift. He believed the repercussions of this accommodationism were often subtle but influential even in the church today, as we shall see in the next section. It is these repercussions that were

---

18. Sider, *To See History Doxologically*, 101–2.

19. Yoder, "Historiography as a Ministry to Renewal," 217.

20. Yoder, "Historiography as a Ministry to Renewal," 216. Conceiving of history in the form of remembrance could lead to a primitive history of decline, according to which everything was good in the early church but then it went downhill for the next two thousand years. Yet Yoder was aware of this danger, and he maintained that also the early church was flawed and the church at no point in history had gotten it right in every regard; see Paddison, review of *To See History Doxologically*, 390. Yoder describes his Radical Reformation vision of the church in this way: "In fact, in contrast to other views of the church, this is one which holds more strongly than others to a positive doctrine of fallibility. Any existing church is not only fallible but in fact peccable." See Yoder, *Priestly Kingdom*, 5.

the main interest in Yoder's treatment of the Constantinian shift. Yoder was not overly concerned with the specifics of the historical events surrounding the Constantinian shift; rather, he was interested in the changed ethos in that church he believed came with the Constantinian shift. A poignant quotation from Yoder makes this interest clear:

> By the label Constantinian we refer less to the man Constantine than to the period, although the man did more than any other person to consummate the change. He was not the only architect of the change; it had begun before him and was not complete until a century after him. It amounted to a fundamental reorientation in the relationship of church and world.[21]

Alexander Sider utilizes a term from Gadamer to explain how Yoder's main interest lay in how the Constantinian shift became "historically effective."[22] Yoder was thus interested in an ethos, in the effects of the Constantinian shift for the church.

In response to what Yoder interpreted as the decline of the church in the Constantinian shift he developed an ecclesiology, according to which the church must resist the temptation of compromising the lordship of Christ; a temptation arising with the church entering into union with the secular powerbrokers. Instead the church must follow the pattern of Christian discipleship that extends to all aspects of life. By doing so the church becomes a political witness, since Yoder holds "the politics of Jesus" to consist in a distinct form of communal life rather than a traditional political standpoint.

The Politics of Jesus is also the title of Yoder's most recognized book.[23] In this book, Yoder argued against the so-called realist position of (the Lutheran) Reinhold Niebuhr (1892–1971). Theological "realists" like Reinhold Niebuhr argued that it was a necessity for Christians to partake in wars, for only in that way could they take responsibility in society.[24] And since the

---

21. Yoder, *Christian Attitudes to War, Peace, and Revolution*, 57.

22. Sider, *To See History Doxologically*, 129.

23. Yoder, *Politics of Jesus*. First published in 1972. Jürgen Moltmann wrote the preface to a German translation, which he found it was already high time for when it came out in 1981: "Mit der längst fälligen deutschen Übersetzung dieses Buches von John Yoder kommt endlich die mennonitische 'täuferische' und friedenskirchliche Stimme in unseren gegenwärtigen theologischen und politischen Diskussionen zu Gehör." See Yoder 2012, xiii. Moltmann goes on to point out that it is about time the four-hundred-year-old European prejudice against the Radical Reformation churches comes to an end.

24. Harold Bender most probably played a role in forming Yoder's view on how

gospels did not take into account the nation states, the gospels could not be used as guidance in such matters. Against this Yoder argued that the portraits of Jesus in the gospels are not just of a guru teaching personal salvation but of a rabbi taking the very political position of pacifism. Yoder argued that to follow the calling to pacifism would eventually always be the more responsible thing to do; as opposed to Christians attempting to take charge of the development of society. For Yoder following what he believed was the calling of the church to pacifism was the only responsible action to take, and only through its concrete presence as an alternative community could the church truly serve as a witness to the world.[25] It ought not to come as a surprise then that Yoder interpreted the Constantinian shift as a heresy, which betrayed both the ethical and the eschatological character of the church.[26] An analysis of how Yoder reached such an interpretation of the Constantinian shift will follow in the next section.

The way Yoder conceived of the theological task differs from how theology is often done in the academy in the Western world today, and he is therefore easy to dismiss.[27] But Yoder also forces one to ask different questions and approach theology differently, which can be a cumbersome process, but thus the more rewarding, as will become evident in the following.[28]

Lutheran theology is different from Anabaptist theology; "Bender clearly distinguished Anabaptism's emphasis on the 'transformation of life through discipleship' from the alleged Lutheran focus on 'enjoyment of the inner experience of the Grace of God through faith.'" See Finger, "Anabaptism and Eastern Orthodoxy," 71.

25. Huebner and Hauerwas, *Precarious Peace*, 58.

26. Nikolajsen, *Distinctive Identity of the Church*, 105. Yoder is using "heresy" in a way not referring directly to the lack of orthodoxy but rather to the lack of orthopraxy, which developed in the church around the Constantinian shift.

27. Alexander Sider, who did his doctorate on Yoder's understanding of history, makes this point thus bluntly: "To the extent that I am correct, ecclesially mainstream theologians and historians will not be compelled to take non-Constantinian theologies seriously." See Sider, "Constantinianism before and after Nicea," 139.

28. This challenge has been taken up increasingly within theology in the English-speaking world. Jeppe Bach Nikolajsen has compiled a list of twelve dissertations published in various countries written on the theology of Yoder within the last thirty years. Though not an exhaustive list, it does witness to the interest in Yoder' theology, see Nikolajsen, "Redefining the Identity of the Church," 16.

4.2 Yoder's Interpretation of the Constantinian Shift

Yoder never produced a systematic tome, but published a wide range of essays addressing various issues. Consequently, his writing is spread out over a number of publications, and so his interpretation of the Constantinian shift has to be traced down through a number of different sources.[29] Furthermore, his writings often is a blend of an analysis of historical events and of a contemporary situation. In order to arrive at a well-rounded representation of Yoder's interpretation of the Constantinian shift it has thus become necessary to glean from a number of essays. I have here provided an outline of the three essays on which I have predominantly relied. These are the essays in which Yoder most succinctly expresses his interpretation of the Constantinian shift.[30]

Subsequently I will analyze Yoder's interpretation of the Constantinian shift through exploring main themes in his essays, pertaining to questions also dealt with by Eusebius and Augustine. After that it will be possible to move on to a preliminary conclusion on Yoder's interpretation of the Constantinian shift.

4.2.1 Three Essays in Outline

4.2.1.1 "THE CONSTANTINIAN SOURCES OF WESTERN SOCIAL ETHICS"

The essay "The Constantinian Sources of Western Social Ethics" was published as chapter 7 of *The Priestly Kingdom* in 1984.[31] Yoder is here laying out how he views the early church living by an ethic attuned to life in a hostile world. Christians today, Yoder argues, are living in a world committed to other values than the church, but the church today is not upholding an ethic like that of the early church. Yoder believes this lack of a development of a contemporary theology adequate to the changing context can

---

29. Stanley Hauerwas has quipped on Yoder's publication style: "I once thought no one could publish more obscurely than I have. But reading through [Mark] Nation's book and his extensive bibliography of Yoder's work, I know my claim to obscurity to be sheer pretension." See Nation, *John Howard Yoder*, x–xi.

30. For an account of which essays and books of Yoder's have come to gain the most influence, see Martens, *Heterodox Yoder*, 1. Yoder often reiterated his points of views and he remained "remarkably consistent over the course of a long career." See Dula and Huebner, *New Yoder*, ix.

31. Yoder, *Priestly Kingdom*.

be traced back to a shift in mentality that happened in the church with the Constantinian shift. This shift is what he sets out to investigate.

Yoder begins by pointing out that this is not a study concerned with the man Constantine, but rather with the new epoch in Christianity that he came to symbolize. Yoder sketches out how a different ethical system appeared after the Constantinian shift, an ethic which can be summarized as asking what best supported the existing political and social structures. Yoder then lays out how this new accommodationist theological ethic manifested itself in a number of ways throughout church history.

Yoder ends his essay by concluding that the mental shift that occurred in the church with Constantine is still prevalent and explains why the ethics and life of the church today is not closer to the early church than is the case. This is why many attempts to renew Christian thought regarding its participation in power structures of the state has not managed to break free of the thought patterns of the Constantinian shift.

4.2.1.2 "The Meaning of the Constantinian Shift"

The essay "The Meaning of the Constantinian Shift" (2009) first appeared in print in 1983, as part of the published lecture-notes on a course taught by Yoder on the Yale historian Roland Bainton's 1960 book *Christian Attitudes toward War and Peace*.[32] In this essay Yoder asks what the Constantinian shift is and how it affects the church today.

Yoder structures the essay in three main parts. In the first part, Yoder explains how the church went from being persecuted to being privileged. The church had grown to a size, where it was more beneficial for the emperor to make an alliance with the church than to persecute it. As a result of the Roman Empire's openness to Christianity, new possibilities arose and it became possible for Christians to be in the military and take public offices. The church regarded this as a triumph, but it came at the cost of the original

---

32. Bainton, *Christian Attitudes toward War and Peace*. Bainton himself hailed from a pacifist family and understood the church before the Constantinian shift to have adhered to a pacifist ethic. Yoder generally agreed with Bainton's historical account: "The age of persecution down to the time of Constantine was the age of pacifism to the degree that during this period no Christian author to our knowledge approved of Christian participation in battle. The position of the Church was not absolutist, however. There were some Christians in the army and they were not on that account excluded from communion." See Bainton, *Christian Attitudes toward War and Peace*, 66. Like Bainton Yoder did not deny that there were Christians in the military, but Yoder did not interpret that as the normative stand of the early church.

ethics of a church, which now had to change in order to be responsible for keeping up the empire.

In the second part of the essay, Yoder describes how the Constantinian shift came to have theological implications. Yoder points out how what most fundamentally changed was the way God's working in history was perceived. Yoder argues that after the Constantinian shift the Roman Empire was perceived as the place where God's will was carried out instead of the church. Therefore a whole new theology became necessary, and the works of pagan writers like Cicero were utilized to formulate this new accommodated theology.

In the third part of the essay, Yoder explains how the theory of just war sprang out of a church accommodating to the requirements of the Roman Empire. Instead of the church bridging the divide between human beings that was instituted in the form of empires and states, the church instead came to serve these divides by legitimizing the wars that upheld the structures of empires and states. The development of a theological theory of just war Yoder sees as the epitome of a church having left its original beliefs and taken over a Constantinian ethic.

4.2.1.3 "Peace Without Eschatology"

The essay "Peace Without Eschatology" was first published in 1954 for a theological conference in Zeist in the Netherlands.[33] In this essay, Yoder responds to the claim that Christian pacifism is an irresponsible way of being in the world, since pacifism fails to take into account the responsibility for the innocent people who will come to suffer if no one stands up to violently fight an oppressor.[34] Against this claim Yoder recasts the question of how responsible behavior of the church looks like and argues that it is only when Christians forget the meaning of eschatology that they can come to think the responsible action of the church will be to participate in violence.

---

33. Yoder, *Royal Priesthood*. It subsequently came to be published as chapter 3 of Yoder's book *The Original Revolution*.

34. A point of view formulated most succinctly by Luther in his *Von Weltlicher Obrigkeit, wie weit man ihr Gehorsam schuldig sei* from 1523. The responsibility for the weak is the argument Luther uses to justify the first use of the law and subsequently a military apparatus. Characteristically, Luther is here uttering a normative claim for all of society, and not just for how the church ought to act in the world; the quintessence of a Constantinian approach to the task of a theologian, from Yoder's perspective

Yoder begins by describing how Jesus was not violent, not even against his oppressors. This led to his crucifixion but also his exaltation. Thus the most responsible way Christians are to be in the world is to be obedient to Christ's example of non-violence, as the only way to defeat evil is to resist the temptation to meet it on its own terms.

Yoder moves on to describe what peace without eschatology looks like. Yoder describes how the "Constantinian heresy" became the result of a theology, which had forgotten about eschatology.[35] Yoder characterizes such a form of Christianity as ultimately a tribal religion that wants God to fight for the empire; the prospering of the state or the empire is equaled with the prospering of Christianity. Yoder argues that when the church forgets that God is ultimately in control of history, it thinks it has to take over the control of the world.

Yoder points out that the claim that Christians have a responsibility to participate in violent structures in order to take care of an innocent third party is a point of view arising only when the church forgets that the most responsible way of being in the world is to follow the example of Christ, as God is the one truly in control of history. Yoder argues that the way of life that would proceed from taking seriously God's rule of history would deny: that the life of the aggressor is worth less than that of the attacked, that the responsibility to prevent evil is an expression of love (when it involves the death of the aggressor), that letting evil happen is as blameworthy as committing it and that the lives of one's own family are worth more than that of an attacker. Yoder knows such statements are scandalous, yet, he argues, the cross has always been interpreted as a scandal in the eyes of the world.

4.2.2 *The Constantinian Shift and Its Theological Consequences*

According to Yoder, the last major persecution of Christians occurred between 305 and 311. At that time, the church had grown so much that Christians constituted a real threat to the empire due to their numerical strength.[36] Constantine realized how persecuting the church would not work, and thus joining them would prove the better strategy. Yoder be-

---

35. Here Yoder defines Constantinianism as "the conception of Christianity that took shape in the century between the Edict of Milan and the City of God." See Yoder, *Royal Priesthood*, 153–54.

36. Yoder, *Christian Attitudes to War, Peace, and Revolution*, 57. Yoder's historical analysis partly relied on outdated literature, and his historical analysis is at places inaccurate.

lieved Constantine did not seem to have undergone a subjective religious conversion, but made Christianity his religion since it would fit better his needs. This change, Yoder believed, was not for the good of the church. How Yoder interpreted the Constantinian shift and how he thought it affected the life and decision-making of the church in general is what we will look at first, before moving into a detailed analysis of how Yoder believed it affected the church within the areas of theological authority, ecclesiology, and eschatology.

The interest for Yoder was not the historical details of Constantine's conversion or the exact number of Christians but rather how the alignment of the church and the Roman Empire led to the development of a changed behavior of Christians. After the Constantinian shift, Christians suddenly found themselves in offices of the administration or serving in the army. This new situation, according to Yoder, led the church to desire the development of an ethic, which allowed Christians to carry out the often violent duties of the empire. Another form of ethic than what the church had lived by earlier came into being. Yoder described it as a drastic shift that he believed opened up to an influx of Roman pagan ideas into Christian theology: "Because Christianity did not have any sources suited to creating such an ethic, it had to be developed by thinkers who used sources they borrowed from the Roman heritage, especially from Cicero."[37]

Yoder believed the biblical Scriptures to be political in nature, but he did also hold the view that they did not offer many resources for the church to develop an ethic, which would accommodate a close connection to the empire, as the biblical Scriptures had arisen in a very different context.[38]

---

37. Yoder, *Christian Attitudes to War, Peace, and Revolution*, 58.

38. In *The Politics of Jesus*, Yoder shows how Jesus' message is intrinsically political, in that it has a broad range of consequences for the power structures and political decisions as to whether to kill people or not. Yoder thus explains why this was not properly acknowledged at his time: "One of the strands in the argument against the normative claims made by or for Jesus has always been that his radical personalism is not relevant to problems of power and structure. Sometimes this ground for rejection has been covered over by more evident arguments such as the 'interim' theme, which says that the ethic of Jesus is disqualified because he expected history not to continue very long. Other times it is shoved aside by the 'elenchtic' theme, that the high demands of the ethic of Jesus are meant not to be obeyed but to bring us to sorrow for our sin. . . . It has nothing to do with the structures of society." See Yoder, *Politics of Jesus*, 134. Yoder holds Bultmann to be one of the foremost proponents of what Yoder labels a grave misunderstanding of the gospel message.

Yoder's interpretation of the Constantinian shift differed from Eusebius's interpretation in regard to the view on the alignment of the ethic of the empire and the church. For Eusebius, the ethics of the Roman Empire and the ethics of the church were mostly aligned, whereas, for Yoder, the ethics of the church and the ethics of the Roman Empire were often at odds. According to Yoder, Augustine re-worked Cicero's ethic to become an ethic for Christian political officials; a claim with some truth to it, as we saw how Augustine's writing was influenced by a number of pagan writers, not least Cicero. What we see here is the outworking of Yoder's Radical Reformation theology, according to which the church was morally better, before it became influenced by the ethics of pagan philosophy. Whether Augustine did in fact "import" a pagan ethics without holding Christ and his example as the final arbiter for it, is not to be judged here. The question that remains and that sums up many of the questions of how to theologically interpret the Constantinian shift, is the principal question of whether a shift in circumstances necessitates a different theological ethic or if the church should always stick to the example of how the early church existed in the world?

Yoder takes the position that the life of the early church, where the church was critical toward the empire, is to be held up as an ideal. But an influence from pagan philosophy instead instilled a new secular authority for the church, Yoder argued, and the needs of the Roman Empire came to govern the ethics of the church. Yoder claimed that this location of a theological authority outside of the church formed a sort of double vision for Christians after the Constantinian shift:

> They [the churches] began to believe that God does some things through the emperor and that God does other things through Christians. God keeps one kind of peace through the emperor and creates other kinds of peace through Christians; the two complement each other. When that duality is in place, that ghetto vision of the necessity of civil authority in wider society, then Christians are prepared to say that when Caesar converts to Christianity, God will use him as a converted Caesar—not to be a king like Jesus but to be a ruler who favors the Christians.[39]

I believe these sentences point to general structures in Yoder's interpretation of the Constantinian shift in at least three ways. I will first lay out these three points and then analyze what they tell us about Yoder's

---

39. Yoder, *Christian Attitudes to War, Peace, and Revolution*, 58–59.

interpretation of the Constantinian shift, before moving into a detailed analysis of specific aspects of Yoder's thought.

First of all it says something about how for Yoder there is such a thing as a specific Christian ethics, which is different from a general ethics of pagan society; for Yoder a Christian ethics is predominantly defined by pacifism. The question as to whether such a thing as a specific Christian ethics exists becomes decisive for Yoder's interpretation of the Constantinian shift. For Yoder, a specific Christian ethics and form of life exists different from that of the wider population; most clearly visible in the early Christians' attitude toward war. Since there is a specific Christian ethics (which in its content is different from the ethics of pagan philosophy) then the Constantinian shift comes to mean that the ethics of the church gets corrupted. For Yoder, this corruption is exemplified in how what we today would term a pacifist witness of the early church stands in a stark contrast to the just war theories, which he identifies with the church after Constantine. In that way the quotation above reveals how Yoder interprets the Constantinian shift as a decline from a better ethics.

Second, the quotation reveals how Yoder believed that after the Constantinian shift, the church understood itself as loyal to a nation-state instead of being an over-national institution not limited by human made lines of demarcation like national borders. For Yoder, the problem of the Constantinian shift was one of loyalty; the Constantinian shift meant that the church was suddenly more loyal to the empire than to what Yoder identified as the over-national nature of the gospel. Yoder's Radical Reformation theology here comes to expression, as this theology strove for a reformation not only in regard to theology and structures of the church but a reformation of all societal structures.

Third, the quotation reveals how Yoder interpreted the Constantinian shift as a story of decline in regard to the church's understanding of the gospel message. For Yoder the Constantinian shift led Christians into the misunderstanding, first described in the gospels: that the Messiah would be a political ruler in the traditional meaning of the term. According to Yoder, the Constantinian shift gave rise to a resurgence of this line of thought. In that sense the Constantinian shift reinvigorated a mistaken theology from the very first gatherings of Christians. This mistaken theology, Yoder maintained, is what led the church to a position of unison with the world, which blinded it from seeing how the violence of the state is deeply contrary to Christian ethics. Yoder did not believe that the church ought not be political, though. According to Yoder the church ought to be political in a far more substantial way than the traditional meaning of the term "political." According to Yoder the church is to be an expression of a different way of being in the world. The church is to consist of a people, who expresses power through service rather than through domination and a people who solves conflicts through forgiveness rather than the sword.[40]

The Constantinian shift was, for Yoder, not only a question of a historical development in the relationship between the state and the church, but rather a question of theology. Yoder identified with the Constantinian shift a theology that he believed misunderstood what it meant that God was the ruler of the world. Yoder interpreted the Constantinian shift as a failed theological interpretation of the right relationship of the church in the world, and he believed that the ethic which became dominant in the church after the Constantinian shift was in fact not derived from theological authorities.[41] The main problem was not as such that the new ethic was inspired by a Roman ethic, but rather that it was adopted without holding Christ as the main arbiter, and thus only accommodated the needs of the empire. Yoder believed this general change resulted in a transformation within the areas of theological authority, ecclesiology and eschatology. How Yoder understood these changes and how they were related to the Constantinian shift I will now look into in more detail.

4.2.3 The Constantinian Shift and Theological Authority

The Constantinian shift, Yoder argued, led to a shift in what authorities the church relied on. Yoder was broadly ecumenical in his outlook on what constituted the theological authorities of the church: Scripture and tradition. How Yoder believed that the practice of the church regarding the use of these changed after the Constantinian shift—specifically how he read Augustine to be responsible for this change—is what I will look at here.

Yoder did not have any one way of reading Scripture, but aimed to exercise creativity in the ways he read Scripture.[42] Yoder maintained the historical reality of Jesus but was not a historical literalist in his reading of

---

40. Yoder, *Politics of Jesus*, 131.

41. Exactly wherein "the theological authorities" for church and theology consist is of course a theological debate in itself. How Yoder answered this question we will also look into in chapter 4.2.3.

42. Nikolajsen, "Menighedens liv med Bibelen," 9.

Scripture.⁴³ Yoder believed that Scripture was at the same time a historical and a normatively authoritative text, which ought to be read in the community of the church, in order to be applied at the contemporary situation in which the church found itself.⁴⁴ The biblical Scriptures ultimately gained their normative status from being canonized by the church, rather than on their own integral authority. When Yoder points to Jesus as the model peacemaker this is done not based on the historical authority of Scripture, but rather on the authority the church has ascribed to it. Yoder believed that when the "dead" debates over the exact historicity of Scripture is set aside "the capacity of the text to speak on topics of war, peace, and revolution increases qualitatively."⁴⁵

The problem for Yoder did not consist in the church not believing in a historical accuracy of Scripture, but rather that the church stopped holding the witness of Scripture as an authority for how to live life. Thereby a discrepancy arose between how Christian life was described in Scripture and how it actually looked. Yoder argued Neo-Platonism was utilized in order to explain this tension between the empirical church and the scriptural vision of the church.⁴⁶ Yoder argued that Augustine especially construed a whole new Neo-Platonist theology that merged the Christian tradition and the common sense of the day. His treatment of Augustine brings us to the center of Yoder's problem with the fourth and fifth-century interpretations of the Constantinian shift:

> Augustine's thought is a consensus kind of moral thought. (. . .) It just asks, does that make sense to all of us? Is that part of our cultural agreement? (. . .) Religion celebrates the unity of everything and the way things are. In the later effort to try to understand this kind of system in terms of comparative religion, some people used the synthetic term ontocracy. Things are ruled by the way they are. The way they are is the way God wants them.⁴⁷

What Yoder describes here is what can be referred to as the naturalistic fallacy; to draw a conclusion from "is" to "ought." I read Yoder as accusing the early interpretations of the Constantinian shift to be guilty of such a fallacy. In Yoder's reading of Eusebius and Augustine they elevated the

43. Yoder, "Use of the Bible in Theology."
44. Nikolajsen, "Menighedens liv med Bibelen," 10–11.
45. Yoder, *Christian Attitudes to War, Peace, and Revolution*, 312.
46. Yoder, *Christian Attitudes to War, Peace, and Revolution*, 63.
47. Yoder, *Christian Attitudes to War, Peace, and Revolution*, 64–65.

current state of affairs for the church into theology, instead of letting the authorities of Scripture and tradition set the course for the church.

The persecutions of Radical Reformation churches in post-Reformation Europe do bear witness as to why Mennonites historically developed a strong suspicion of the idea of a church having a close relationship to the state.[48] I am not convinced, though, that the Mennonite influence regarding suspicion of a strong church-state relation explains all that is going on in Yoder's rejection of the naturalistic fallacy. The inspiration from Karl Barth exerts its influence too. That Yoder did not want the "consensus kind of moral thought" to influence the ethics of the church does resemble a Barthian critique of liberal theology. In the same way that Barth did not want the moral sentiments of society to determine theology, Yoder did not want the consensus of society to influence the ethics of the church.[49] Yoder in that way took Barth's criticism of German Liberal Theology back to the fourth century. Yoder uses the same logic as Barth but locates the starting point of the problem all the way back with the Constantinian shift. Yoder's historical analysis can thereby be viewed as an attempt to improve Barth's critique by getting to the starting point of where the problem of theological "ontocracy" had begun.

Aside from illuminating Yoder's view on authority within theology, the above quotation also reveals how Yoder was a bad reader of Augustine. Yoder did not properly understand Augustine and even lumped Augustine's and Eusebius's interpretations of the Constantinian shift into one.[50] How it effects Yoder's wider theological argument that he was a bad reader of Augustine I will treat in detail in the section on the contemporary cri-

---

48. The first persecutions of Anabaptists occurred already in 1525, and one of the first to die for the new expression of faith was the Anabaptist Hippolytus Eberle. Yoder wrote chapter 3 in Cornelius Dyck's introduction to Mennonite history, and here Yoder refers to Eberle to be known as the first Protestant martyr. See Dyck, *Introduction to Mennonite History*, 54. It does seem, though, that Yoder thereby forgets about Johann Esch and Heinrich Voes, who were executed for their Lutheran beliefs already in 1523.

49. A thorough study on how much Barth did or did not influence Yoder would prove beneficial for the understanding of Yoder's theological project. Nikolajsen believes Barth's influence on Yoder is often overestimated; Yoder was always highly critical toward Barth's view on war, and they never did develop a good personal relationship. See Yoder, *Royal Priesthood*, 166. It is a fact, though, that they both structured their theology around the revelation of Christ, and both were critical toward any form of natural theology. See Nikolajsen, *Distinctive Identity of the Church*, 97.

50. Peter Leithart states that "Yoder's scattered comments on Augustine are among the worst moments in his writing." See Leithart, *Defending Constantine*, 284.

tique on Yoder, as it raises the more fundamental question of the relationship between his historical scholarship and his theological claims.[51] For all of the three interpretations of the Constantinian shift examined in this book, their historical interpretation and their theological claims have been inseparable, and as we saw both Eusebius and Augustine wanted to use historical studies as a tool for theological teaching rather than just being *scriptores*. But can a contemporary theologian present an account of history in the same manner as the earlier masters and still be within a theological academic standard?—I will get to this. It can be concluded here that Yoder believed that the Constantinian shift resulted in the authorities of the church undergoing a change. The way of life depicted in Scripture was no longer understood to be applicable, and the tradition of the early church's radical form of life was neglected. This change had effects for both ecclesiology and eschatology, which is what I will now look into.

4.2.4 The Constantinian Shift and the Understanding of Ecclesiology

Yoder argued that a neo-platonic influence on theology, brought about by the Constantinian shift, led to the church being interpreted as invisible, in a way very different from the witness of the New Testament. Yoder states: "before Constantine, Christians knew as a fact of experience that there was a church, and they had to take it on faith that God governs history. After Constantine, Christians knew for a fact that God governs history (Constantine was one of their number, after all), but they had to take it on faith that there is a church."[52]

According to Yoder it was the Constantinian shift that led the theology of the invisible church to come about. After the Constantinian shift suddenly "the visible church was everybody, because everybody was

---

51. The following paradigmatic quotation reveals how Yoder collapses the Eusebian and the Augustinian interpretation of the Constantinian shift into one: "In short, New Testament Christians knew for a fact that God uses the church for ministries of proclamation, service, and fellowship, but they had to take it on faith that God governs the world. *Eusebius's understandings*. After Constantine, this faith fundamentally changed. Eusebius and Augustine, the two great minds of the fourth and early fifth centuries, worked out an alternative: God governs history through Constantine. In their interpretation." See Yoder, *Christian Attitudes to War, Peace, and Revolution*, 61–62.

52. Yoder, *Christian Attitudes to War, Peace, and Revolution*, 63.

baptized (except a few Jews, who did not count)."[53] As the empire's hospitality toward Christianity filled up the church with insincere believers, a new ecclesiology that accounted for the lack of any moral change in the life of the believers had to be constructed, Yoder argues. It was Augustine who fulfilled this task according to Yoder. Augustine took an approach typical for a Neo-Platonist thinker: He found refuge in referring to dualities and invisibility when encountering a tough problem in the material world. Augustine utilized such a reasoning to explain how what one sees in the visible church does not correspond to what is ultimately real. With such a move, it was no longer impossible to explain how members of the visible church after the Constantinian shift no longer lived lives characterized by the love of neighbor, since Christianity had become an internal decision, and nobody could therefore know who was actually a member of the true invisible church.[54] The marks of the true church now shifted from being congregations living virtuously to being the offices of the church. After the Constantinian shift the true church was characterized as the institution, where the officials had been properly ordained. Yoder pointed out, though, that the neo-platonic way of thinking permeated all levels of Augustine's thinking, so that it could not be decided whether members of the visible priesthood were members of the real church, as priests and bishops could be hypocrites like anyone else. As not even the holders of offices were signs of a true church the end result was that the church became completely elusive in respect to consisting of human beings and instead became perceived only in abstract terms.[55]

Yoder used his interpretation of the Constantinian shift to utter a critique of the present-day church that did not live up to his Radical Reformation ideals of church. The emphasis on the dogma of the invisible church would inevitably create problems for Yoder: as we saw, he believed the church ought to serve the world by standing out as an example of a virtuous community. If the church is invisible such an ecclesiology will hardly make sense, as there can be no church to point to as the virtuous example for the world. Yoder connected this critique of the dogma of the invisible church with the historical event of the Constantinian shift.

This critique of Augustine might not be fair, though. It is true that Augustine played a part in the process to internalize Christianity, but, as we

53. Yoder, *Christian Attitudes to War, Peace, and Revolution*, 62.
54. Yoder, *Christian Attitudes to War, Peace, and Revolution*, 62.
55. Yoder, *Christian Attitudes to War, Peace, and Revolution*, 63.

saw in part 3, for Augustine this internalization of Christianity did not lead to an ecclesiology less critical of the empire; in fact the opposite took place. Augustine wanted to save the church from being identified with the empire, and the concept of the invisible church was exactly a way through which to accomplish this. Only during the Reformation, as a polemical argument against the Catholic Church, was the concept of the invisible church developed further by the reformers, and the invisible church became detached from semblance to the concrete institutional church. Only when the connection to the life and community of the church is severed, does it present an acute problem for Yoder's ecclesiology. Yoder is not giving a proper account of this historical development, as his objective of critiquing a present day church leads him to present a one-sided reading of Augustine. These short comments here only as an introduction to the later critical examination of Yoder's historical scholarship.

The problematic ecclesiology Yoder identified as a consequence of the Constantinian shift was for him tied up closely with how the Constantinian shift led to a flawed understanding of eschatology.

4.2.5 The Constantinian Shift and the Understanding of Eschatology

According to Yoder's reading of the New Testament, God works in the world in two ways: (a) God works through the church. Yoder interprets the church as "an organ of the work of God in history" both now and in the *eschaton*.[56] Its celebration is visible and its confession is public, and with God working through this visible confessing community. (b) God works invisibly. Sitting at the right hand of the father, the risen Christ influences the course of history, but it is not for human beings to discern how.[57] According to Yoder, Eusebius and Augustine agreed on a different view on history. They shared the view that God governs history through Constantine; through the secular ruler.[58] They thereby turned the empire into the church. Their wrong understanding of how God acts in history thereby led to a problematic ecclesiology.

What Yoder criticizes is how what in the early church belonged to the "not yet" was pulled into the "already" when the Constantinian shift

---

56. Yoder, *Christian Attitudes to War, Peace, and Revolution*, 61.
57. Yoder, *Christian Attitudes to War, Peace, and Revolution*, 61.
58. Yoder, *Christian Attitudes to War, Peace, and Revolution*, 61.

was interpreted as the realization of God's kingdom on earth. The church's contribution to and support of the empire was an attempt to force through God's plan for the world; something which ought to be left to God.[59] In theological debates, Radical Reformation theology is often accused of wanting to realize in the "already" what only belongs to the "not yet"; wanting to create the kingdom of heaven on earth. Yoder turned this accusation around, and accused the theologians advocating a "realist" political position of being the ones, who did not adequately understand that to realize with power the agenda of the gospel was something that only belonged to God's judgment in the eschatological future of the church.

It can be concluded that Yoder held the Constantinian shift to be a change in regard to theological authority, the ethics of the church, and the understanding of eschatology. In regard to the latter Yoder said the church (after the Constantinian shift) began to hold the presupposition that it was up to human beings to decide the fate of this world; something Yoder believed helped lead to the development of theological theories of just war.

What Yoder's account of the development of the theory of just war tells about his interpretation of the Constantinian shift I will look into in the following.

4.2.6 The Constantinian Shift and the Emergence of the Theory of Just War

Pacifism is one of the central tenants in Yoder's theology. Not because Yoder held pacifism to be the more efficient strategy to avoid wars in general (Yoder had no such illusions), but he held pacifism to be the proper Christian response to the gospel message.[60] He pointed out that for the church to follow the biblical call to pacifism was very difficult after the Constantinian shift. Therefore the teaching of just war became necessary for the church. According to Yoder the theory of just war did not derive from Scripture or from the tradition of the church, but began as a convenient stance, only to be somewhat systematized by Thomas Aquinas long after the Constantinian shift. All undertaken in order to theologically justify the state of things; to provide theological justification to the existence of nation-states and wars.[61]

---

59. Yoder, *Priestly Kingdom*, 136–37.
60. Yoder, *Royal Priesthood*, 145.
61. Yoder, *Christian Attitudes to War, Peace, and Revolution*, 66–67.

Yoder argued that what facilitated the development of the theory of just war was the fact that the church had become mainstream after the Constantinian shift. Yoder interpreted the church abandoning the call of pacifism as the core example of the corrupting effects of the Constantinian shift on the church. On three areas pertaining to moral conduct the church changed. As far as they cast light on Yoder's interpretation of the Constantinian shift, I will now examine these assumed moral changes.

After the Constantinian shift the emperor was now a member of the church. That was a novel situation for the church to find itself in. According to Yoder's analysis, the church quickly arrived at the insight that it could not advise the emperor to act like Jesus. Why would that not be a viable way for the church? Yoder believed that the church reasoned that the emperor's behavior would lead to a Christian emperor not being the emperor for a very long time, constituting a problem for a church that understood itself to be responsible for how history developed, and being afraid of persecution. According to Yoder, the church reasoned it was more important that the emperor was a Christian than it was to follow the right ethic.[62] The theology after the Constantinian shift dictated that God wanted the emperor to be a Christian, so what had to be done by the emperor in order to maintain his position the church did not condemn. According to Yoder, helping the Christian empire to achieve success became construed as God's cause after the Constantinian shift.[63]

Yoder used his analysis of a changed ethic and a changed eschatological vision to argue against the theory of just war. In Yoder's interpretation of the Constantinian shift, the problem of an erroneous praxis of the church was closely connected to the problem of an erroneous teaching. It was not that the church had a wrong understanding of ethics, which then allowed the emergence of the theory of just war. It was rather that the church had a practice of accommodating to the empire, which led to an erroneous theory, like that of just war, to emerge.

The second moral change was that the church after the Constantinian shift did not offer guidance to a single individual who had taken the risk of turning Christian, but was offering guidance to a whole culture. Yoder explained how the morality of the early Christians was heroic; since they were ready to be thrown to the lions. But after the Constantinian shift everybody

---

62. Yoder, *Christian Attitudes to War, Peace, and Revolution*, 70.
63. Yoder, *Royal Priesthood*, 154.

was part of the church, and the church was not persecuted anymore.[64] According to Yoder's understanding of the pre-Constantinian church a very different ethics governed the church before the Constantinian shift: "The presumption was conversion, a reorientation of all life. The assumption people made on joining the church in the first century was they would take on a whole new set of obligations and a new definition of what it means to do the will of God."[65] It is a fact that joining the church before the Constantinian shift customarily implied undertaking a long catechumenate before baptism, as it was important for the early church to teach people what they were baptized into. Yoder argued that after the Constantinian shift the long catechumenate was no longer expected of people joining the church, as the new situation made a thorough catechumenate superfluous.[66] The church was in a situation that made it necessary to conceive of an ethics that would fit the ordinary person, and not a person who had taken the life-altering choice, which it was to become a Christian in the early church. Only by changing its ethical standards did the church after Constantine make it possible at the same time to be a Christian and a good citizen.

According to Yoder's analysis, the theory of just war is an example of such an accommodation. Participating in wars would be unavoidable for a good citizen and the theological justification of just war opened up for Christian participation in war. Interestingly, Yoder points out that the church continued to hold up an image of what he calls "the heroic vision" of the Christian life in form of the monastic movement.[67] The monastics did not understand themselves as responsible for "running the world" and monasticism thereby served as a reminder of the previous radical Christian movement. In that respect Yoder's historical analysis agrees with also the contemporary scholarship pointing to the growth of the church, and the following cease of persecution, as one of the factors leading to the rise of

---

64. For this statement there is historical basis. Robert Markus puts it thus: "Within a century of Constantine's conversion to Christianity, being a 'Roman' had come to be much the same as being a 'Christian.'" See Markus, *Christianity and the Secular*, 71.

65. Yoder, *Christian Attitudes to War, Peace, and Revolution*, 71.

66. Yoder's historical analysis is strongly driven by his theological program, and he does not support his argument with detailed historical references. For example, he completely ignores the catechetical instruction prescribed by Cyril of Jerusalem (ca. 315–386). That some intellectual training was required as part of joining the church does not substantially weaken Yoder's theological argument much, though, as Yoder's focus was on a lack of orthopraxy being caused by the Constantinian shift, and only secondarily on the lack of orthodoxy.

67. Yoder, *Christian Attitudes to War, Peace, and Revolution*, 72.

the monastic movement.⁶⁸ If the model for the right life of the Christian is depicted as that of a disciplined martyr, then a negative interpretation of the Constantinian shift does seem inevitable.

4.2.7 The Constantinian Shift and the Church as Mainstream Culture

Yoder argues that, before the Constantinian shift, Christianity was a destabilizing force in the Roman Empire whereas after the Constantinian shift, the church gained the religious role of keeping the empire together. Yoder believed that: "the word *religion* is adopted to describe Christianity, which previously did not see itself as one of the religions. Religion is what holds society together."⁶⁹ Yoder's argument runs like this: All societies need religion, as religion functions to hold a society together, because it gives a sense of legitimacy and purpose to wider societal functions. Christianity, Yoder argued, had not served this purpose before the Constantinian shift, but was rather a force of instability. It was only when Christianity came to serve the role of upholder of society that it became a "religion"; at that point the church was no longer an alternative community, but a protector of the mainstream.

Yoder intelligently tied up his interpretation of the changed circumstance of the church after the Constantinian shift with Karl Barth's theological question as to how Christianity is to be understood as a religion.⁷⁰

---

68. For an example of such an account of the rise of the monastic movement, see MacCulloch, *History of Christianity*, 201. Though, already in 1853 Søren Kierkegaard had come to the same explanation of the emergence of the monastic movement: "Forrykkelsen af hele Christendommen. Christendommen degraderes til at blive Stats-Religion. Samtidigt dermed blev Xstd. Doctrin—og Askesen opkom. Askesen er den *situationsløse* Forsagelse, da Xstd. kæmpede og leed Forfølgelse behøvedes Askesen i den Forstand ikke." See Kierkegaard, *Søren Kierkegaards skrifter*, 222. In English: "The displacement of the whole of Christianity. Christianity was degraded into becoming a state religion. At the same time Christianity thereby became a doctrine—and asceticism arose. Asceticism is situationless renunciation. When Christianity battled and suffered persecution, asceticism in this sense was not needed." See Kierkegaard, *Søren Kierkegaard's Journals and Papers*, 71.

69. Yoder, *Christian Attitudes to War, Peace, and Revolution*, 72.

70. Barth famously argued that Christianity certainly is a religion in its human form, but it is also not a religion in that it centers on God's word instead of human beings. Succinctly expressed in his speech "Christianity or Religion?" from 1963. See Barth, *Fragments Grave and Gay*, 27–31.

Yoder's focus on the visible church changed the tone of Barth's statement, though. For Yoder it turned into a criticism not of the way the individual perceived Christianity, but rather a critique of the way the church acts in society. How the church thought about war was also tied up with the concept of religion in Yoder's analysis, since war was thus seen as a necessity and therefore Christianity needed to support it in order to uphold society.[71] Yoder's criticism of "religion" sums up his fundamental problem with a theological theory of just war: After the Constantinian shift the church understood the function of upholding society as more important than pursuing the ethic of Scripture and tradition.

We have seen how the Constantinian shift became a historical lens through which Yoder criticized what happened to the church in the fourth and fifth centuries. But Yoder's interpretation of the Constantinian shift did not only concern what happened hundreds of years ago, as he believed the Constantinian shift to influence church history up until today. How Yoder in four instances traces the outworking in history of the Constantinian shift constitutes the next, and last, theme of the analysis.

4.2.8 The Constantinian Shift and the Contemporary Situation of the Church

Have most churches not long ago left behind the connection between church and state, and thereby made all talk of a contemporary Constantinian situation irrelevant? Yoder would argue the answer is no. The Constantinian way of thinking has become part of the mentality of the Christian West. The story of a post-Constantinian shift mentality is what Yoder traces. But, one might object once again, after the Reformation and the Enlightenment there was a move away from the Constantinian era, and church and state were separated in most parts of the world. Nonetheless, according to Yoder, the Constantinian modes of thought are so deeply engrained that, even when circumstances changed, these ways of thinking lingered on and expressed themselves in a number of neo-Constantinianisms.[72] Yoder thus conceived of the Constantinian shift in changed patterns of thought and behavior, rather than strict historical terms. In the following I will examine how Yoder understood these Constantinian patterns of thought to have reiterated themselves since the fourth century.

71. Yoder, *Christian Attitudes to War, Peace, and Revolution*, 72–73.
72. Yoder, *Priestly Kingdom*, 141.

Was the Reformation a historical event in which political misuse of Christianity was brought to a halt? Yoder did not think so. He believed the Reformation did not mean a reversal of the Constantinian vision but only a recasting of it on a smaller scale; now with the church being loyal toward a number of nation-states instead of just one empire. After the Reformation, it became more important to be Danish, German, French or English, than to be part of the wider unity of the church.[73] The Reformation churches did not manage to properly oppose the idea of loyalty toward the state being stronger than the loyalty toward the church, but instead embraced that way of thinking and organized churches on the national scale. Instead of the church uniting with the one grand empire, it was now just wed to a lot of smaller empires. Whereas wars before had been waged against external enemies, this new situation opened up the possibility of waging wars against other Christian nations.[74] According to Yoder, most Christians adjusted well to the new arrangement. It was easy for the novel Protestant churches to fit into this new political setup, since their ecclesiology from the outset had been tied up with the nation-state, though also the Catholic Church took on a national coloring after the Reformation. Even if the political circumstances changed, the basic Constantinian structures remained, as the close connection between the church and the secular powers were still perceived as the natural order. Yoder refers to this new form of a Constantinian settlement, brought about by the Reformation, as neo-Constantinianism.[75]

Such an account of the Reformation serves as a good example of how Yoder's interpretation of the Constantinian shift is influenced by his Radical Reformation theology, according to which a Reformation without

---

73. Yoder, *Priestly Kingdom*, 141.

74. As an immediate critique of Yoder's thesis, one could point to the fourth crusade and its sack of Constantinople in 1204 as an example of Christian empires engaged in internal war before the formation of the nation-state. It has to be granted to Yoder, though, that Pope Innocent III's multiple condemnations of the participants in the siege of Constantinople shows that at least the pope was aware of the fact that a war against another Christian empire was a highly problematic affair. See Phillips, *Fourth Crusade and the Sack of Constantinople*, 198.

75. Yoder, *Priestly Kingdom*, 142. The opposition to such a national Constantinianism has prompted Stanley Hauerwas, the most renowned theologian influenced by Yoder's ideas, to put on his office door a large poster dictating: "A Modest Proposal for Peace: Let the Christians of the World Agree That They Will Not Kill Each Other." Some will object that Christians ought not to kill anyone—period! Hauerwas can then, based on the tragic history of religious wars between nation-states, pragmatically point out that "well, they do call it a modest proposal."

a political aspect was a Reformation only carried half way through. For Yoder, the Reformation presented a possibility for the church to reconceive its position in relation to the state; and yet the church failed to summon the theological imagination to sufficiently re-interpret the Constantinian shift and break away from the close relationship to the political powers.

During the Enlightenment and the accompanying revolutionary political upheavals, Yoder argued, the Western church had another chance to rethink its position in relation to the state. Albeit the formal institutional connection between church and state was significantly weakened a moral identification between church and state remained. Yoder used the United States as an example, arguing that even though church and state are formally separated in the US, it is still conceived of as a nation structured according to the will of God. The state is perceived to hold a Christian mandate, and the ascription of moral value to the nation thereby continued, even though the church is formally separate from the state. This form of Constantinianism Yoder referred to as neo-neo-Constantinianism.[76]

Yoder pointed to two other ways in which the Constantinian way of thinking had further come to expression during his lifetime. The first was in communist regimes. Even though the communist regime persecuted the church, Christians still remained largely loyal to the nation. The official view of religion from the communist state was that religion would wither away but nevertheless the church still remained loyal to the state and continued to perceive itself as Russian Orthodox. This Yoder referred to as neo-neo-neo-Constantinianism.[77] Another form of Constantinianism Yoder identified in the phenomenon of Christians dreaming of a future political salvation. Such a line of thought expressed itself in neo-Marxist terms at Yoder's time and promised a better and more just political system yet to come, with which Christians should proleptically identify themselves. Thereby identifying salvation only with political change. This Yoder referred to as neo-neo-neo-neo-Constantinianism.[78]

More neo-Constantinianisms have probably sprung up since Yoder's death, but we will stop here, as these examples adequately illustrate how Yoder interpreted the Constantinian shift and identified the ways it had become "historically effective." It can be concluded that Yoder used the term

---

76. Yoder, *Priestly Kingdom*, 142.
77. Yoder, *Priestly Kingdom*, 142.
78. Yoder, *Priestly Kingdom*, 143.

Constantinian shift both to name a historical event and to name a certain mentality in the church after the fourth century.

For Yoder, the Constantinian shift served as the explanation of why there is a grand difference between how Christianity looked in the first centuries and how Christianity looks today.[79] That such a distance exists, Yoder argued, is a sign of apostasy and disavowal. It is a distance that has arisen due to a systemic misconception of the role of the church in the world.[80] Many have tried to mend this misconception and renew Christian thought, but they have been caught in ways of thinking, which belonged to the broken system they meant to reject.

Nevertheless, Yoder's interpretation of the role of the church today is not one of condemnation. He holds that it is possible to conceive of a non-Constantinian church in this day and age, but this will have to take its beginning in the lived life of the church and not in an abstract theory of theology. Yoder argues that is was exactly when the church forgot the Jews, and thereby it's concrete history and link to specific places and events, that it began to compromise its original way of life.[81] Instead of moving into an examination of Yoder's prescriptive theology, I will in the next section sum up how he interpreted the Constantinian shift.

4.2.9 Conclusion

Yoder's engagement with the interpretation of the Constantinian shift was focused on righting a wrong. According to Yoder the Constantinian shift had led to the church forgetting to whom it owed its primary loyalty. His account of the Constantinian shift was not just a historical investigation, but academic work with utmost relevance for the contemporary church.

---

79. This begs the question as to whether the theology and life-form of the early church holds a normative status for contemporary church and theology. For an Anabaptist theologian like Yoder, that is not much of a question, but Christians from other traditions might not agree. Is the upholding of the early church as a theological authority for today maybe failing to take into account how the church must continually change in form and outlook in order to remain faithful to its commission? How one interprets the Constantinian shift is a good indicator of how one thinks about this question, for if the early church is regarded as an authority, then it understandably becomes rather difficult to evaluate positively the shift that changed the life of the church to such a great extent.

80. Yoder, *Priestly Kingdom*, 144.

81. Hauerwas, *Matthew*, 62.

Church and World

The Constantinian shift and the theology which sprang from it had, according to Yoder, led to theological misconceptions that are still influential in the church today. Yoder believed the contemporary situation in the West to bear a strong resemblance to the societal context of the fourth and fifth centuries, and the current situation therefore constituted a unique opportunity for the church to regain what he held to be the right perspective on its role in the world.

The misconceptions Yoder saw springing from the Constantinian shift can be summarized in two main categories. The first being a misunderstanding concerning the relationship between the church and the world. We saw that Yoder found it to be a problematic consequence of the Constantinian shift that the lines between the church and wider society had been blurred. Yoder argued this led to Christians holding not Christ but the common ideas of society as the highest authority, most significantly expressed in the way Christians came to relate to war after the Constantinian shift.

The second being a misunderstanding concerning how to understand who is in charge of history. After the Constantinian shift, success on a political level came to be identified as a realization of God's plan for the world; a mode of thought to be found, for example, in the crusades and in the colonial projects of Western countries.[82] According to Yoder, the church ought instead to serve as an example standing out from the rest of the world in order to point the world toward salvation. Yoder understood the church to be political, simply by being in the world in a different manner, as this often entails a political stance. Yoder considered this different way of being in the world to be a political witness in itself. Instead the political action of the church became tied up with victories of the empire, and salvation became viewed in terms of military victory. Thereby a misunderstanding in regard to how to conceive of history and politics led to a betrayal of the eschatological character of the church.

As Eusebius's and Augustine's interpretations of the Constantinian shift were summed up in five points, so I will use the same categories here: (a) Yoder was driven by a strong theological vision for his work, and his interpretation of the Constantinian shift was determined by this theological program. (b) Though the church ultimately serves the world by its witness in word and deed, Yoder in his interpretation of the Constantinian shift expressed skepticism toward any alignment of the interest of the secular ruler and the church. (c) According to Yoder, the Constantinian shift was not just

---

82. Yoder, *Royal Priesthood*, 154.

a political occurrence, it marked the beginning of a new historical period in the history of the church: the Constantinian Era. (d) Though Yoder did not think it possible to identify occurrences in political history directly instigated by God, he did point out a historical occurence not instigated by God, since he identified the Constantinian shift as such. (e) Yoder did not take the Constantinian shift as evidence that it would go well for Christians in this world. For Yoder, the model of the good life for the Christian was rather connected to the concept of the martyr, who is to bear witness to the sins of the people in power. But the Constantinian shift had made it increasingly difficult for the church to properly identify such sins.

Despite Yoder's pacifism—such an interpretation of the Constantinian shift was an invitation to a fight in the scholarly world. Both in his lifetime and afterwards Yoder received criticism for his interpretation of the Constantinian shift. I will now turn toward this debate.

4.3 The Contemporary Debate

Eusebius of Caesarea provided a theological interpretation of how to understand the Constantinian shift. And, as we saw in the preceding section, Eusebius's interpretation came to be criticized after his death. Yoder's theology is in many respects different from that of Eusebius, but, similar to the fourth-century bishop, Yoder also produced a thorough theological interpretation of the Constantinian shift in a period, where the role of the church has been undergoing change. And Yoder encountered strong criticism for his interpretation of the Constantinian shift too.[83] Most poignantly the theologian and historian Peter Leithart has criticized Yoder on his interpretation of the Constantinian shift.[84] In his 2010 book *Defending Constantine* Peter Leithart sets out to correct Yoder's mistakes; both on a historical and a theological level.[85] The debate seems to be played out in

---

83. Whereas Eusebius's interpretation of the Constantinian shift was contested by Augustine, a re-interpretation of the Constantinian shift of such theological grandeur as found in the *De Civitate Dei* has yet to be presented as a response to Yoder, though.

84. Peter J. Leithart (1959–) is senior fellow of theology at New Saint Andrews College in Idaho. He earned his PhD at Cambridge (directed by John Milbank) in 1998 and has written broadly in systematic and historical theology. Leithart is an ordained minister in the Presbyterian Church in America.

85. In the introduction to *Defending Constantine* Leithart accounts for how Yoder constitutes the main polemical target of his book: "*Constantinianism* is the name given by Yoder, Hauerwas, and their increasing tribe to what they consider a heretical mindset

American theology at the intersection of disciplines of church history and systematic theology.[86]

Yoder's interpretation of the Constantinian shift often falls short in accounting for the positive influence on Western culture by the Christendom, which came into existence during the Constantinian Era. Reading Yoder one can get the impression that the church fell into a slumber from the fourth century onwards, then started to wake up in the sixteenth century but is only now coming to its senses again. As William Cavanaugh has pointed out, such a view of history is, besides from being ignorant to the historical developments in the church, theologically problematic: "If the Holy Spirit did not simply go on holiday during that period [the Constantinian Era], we must find ways to appreciate Christendom."[87] These are the questions Leithart is dealing with in his book. Here I will first look at Leithart's critique of Yoder's historical analysis of the Constantinian shift, and then at Leithart's critique of the theological consequences Yoder draws from his historical analysis.[88]

4.3.1 Criticism of Yoder's Historical Analysis

By criticizing Yoder's historical analysis Leithart naturally comes to stand at odds with most of Yoder's theological thinking, since Yoder's interpretation of the Constantinian shift is foundational for his theology. Leithart accuses Yoder of working with a "prior narrative" of the fall of the church, which he has taken over from sixteenth-century Anabaptist sources. Yoder's interpretation of the Constantinian shift, Leithart argues, comes to work for Yoder in a "mythical fashion" as the prism through which Yoder sees

---

and set of habits that have distorted Christian faith since (at least) the fourth century. Most of my argument is directed at Yoder, who provided the most sophisticated and systematic treatment of the concept." See Leithart, *Defending Constantine*, 10–11.

86. At the AAR (American Academy of Religion) conference in San Francisco in 2011 a session was held on Leithart's *Defending Constantine*, with participants from University of Virginia and Duke Divinity School.

87. Leithart, *Defending Constantine*, see back cover.

88. Leithart's criticism of Yoder cannot be equaled with Augustine's counter-interpretation to Eusebius, but it provides some pointers as to how a contemporary political theology, which at the same time takes into account Yoder's critique of Constantinian modes of thought in Western Christianity and counters the problematic aspects of Yoder's theology, might look like. To be desired is a theological account of the relationship between church and world, which concurrently considers the goodness of the created world and accounts for its fallen condition.

all other aspects of church history.[89] When beginning with such a prior scheme on how to interpret history, Yoder comes to have a preconceived model of the development of history that governs his interpretation of the Constantinian shift.

Whether such a scheme can be viable in theological scholarship, I will soon return to in the next section, but first an examination of the two main points where Leithart finds flaws in Yoder's historical scholarship: his understanding of the early church's stand on pacifism and Yoder's reading of Eusebius and Augustine.

As we saw above, much of Yoder's interpretation of the Constantinian shift as a decline of the church hinges on the claim that the pre-Constantinian church upheld what we today would term a pacifist ethic. Leithart is aware of that and it prompts the following statement:

> My argument does not bear the same burden as Yoder's. Yoder is correct only if he can prove a high degree of early Christian consensus in favor of pacifism. My argument, fortunately, does not have to leap such a high bar. If I can demonstrate that the evidence shows that the pre-Constantinian church uniformly acknowledged the legitimacy of Christian participation in the military, then of course I have shown that there was not a shift of the sort that Yoder claims. There may still have been a shift, as one would expect with a professing Christian running the empire and the army, but it would not be the fundamental change that Yoder claims.[90]

For Leithart, to prove that the church before Constantine was not uniformly against participation in any military activity seems fairly easy. The focus of this book is not the question of whether the early church was in fact pacifist or not, but as far as it pertains to Yoder's interpretation of the Constantinian shift, I will entertain the question here. Leithart points out that, before the mid-second century, it is difficult to establish any numbers regarding Christians being part of the military, but after that time there is a good deal of evidence of Christians fighting in the Roman army.[91] Not only the ordinary people of the early church, but also some of its most important theologians did not condemn war. Tertullian was against Christians participating in wars, and yet the fact that he had to spend so much energy

---

89. Leithart, *Defending Constantine*, 318.
90. Leithart, *Defending Constantine*, 259.
91. Leithart refers to evidence from tomb inscriptions. See Leithart, *Defending Constantine*, 261–65.

on this question serves as evidence that it was a very real practice in the church. Origen, who is often cited as the key proponent of early Christian pacifism, is actually not condemning Caesar's wars as such, but is calling on Christians to pray for the people fighting in the wars, Leithart argues.[92]

Leithart concludes that Yoder's story of a decline of the church from a position of renunciation of violence and war does not hold up. He states: "In short, the story of the church and war is ambiguity before Constantine, ambiguity after, ambiguity right to the present. Constantine is in this respect a far lesser figure than Yoder wants to make him."[93] This view on the question as to whether the church changed its stand on pacifism after the Constantinian shift finds support in an article by Glenn Chesnut on the early Christian historians. When considering the question of violence in the early church Chesnut first states that: "It is probably unfair to argue . . . that the Christians of the first three centuries were pacifists in any modern sense."[94] But then a page later he says that: "Christianity in the first three centuries was, though not totally hostile across the board, at least deeply ambiguous about armies and military service. It was particularly difficult for an early Christian ever to conceive of actually glorifying a warrior figure. The true Christian heroes were the virgins and martyrs."[95] The tension between Chesnut's two statements sums up quite well the stand of the early church regarding the question of violence, and is in line with what Leithart concluded in regard to the church's ambiguity on the question of war.

John D. Roth in 2013 edited the anthology *Constantine Revisited: Leithart, Yoder and the Constantinian Debate,* which contains twelve essays responding to Leithart's critique of Yoder.[96] These essays address many aspects of Leithart's critiques, for example that Leithart fails to account for the liturgical changes taking place around the ascension of Constantine. None of the essays, however, are dedicated to rebut Leithart's claim that the early church did not uniformly hold up a pacifist ideal.[97] If nothing

92. Leithart, *Defending Constantine*, 269.
93. Leithart, *Defending Constantine*, 278.
94. Chesnut, "Eusebius, Augustine, Orosius," 702.
95. Chesnut, "Eusebius, Augustine, Orosius," 703.
96. The authors state openly their adherence (though to varying degree) to Yoder's insights in order to contribute to the conversation in the most honest manner.
97. Multiple of the authors do address the question, though. Alan Kreider's essay "'Converted' but Not Baptized" deals with this question in most detail, as Kreider spends eleven pages on it. He argues that Leithart does not properly acknowledge how, even though the early church was not uniformly pacifist, the writings of Clement of

else the table of contents of that book thus serves as a tacit admission from Yoder's adherents that it is complex to find strong historical evidence for Yoder's claim that pacifism was held up as an ideal in the early church.

Before moving on to consider what this means for Yoder's interpretation of the Constantinian shift I will look at the other important argument Leithart brings to bear against Yoder's historical analysis. When examining the sources Leithart utilizes to mount his critique of Yoder in *Defending Constantine*, it becomes obvious how Leithart has been influenced by the renewed scholarly interest in Eusebius as a theologian.[98] Whereas Yoder, on the other hand, relied on older scholarly literature on Eusebius and the fourth century.[99] In that sense Leithart's book functions as a playing out of the theological consequences of the historians' renewed insights into the nature of Eusebius's work.

Leithart spends the first chapters of his book arguing that Constantine really was a Christian: "Flawed, no doubt, sometimes inconsistent with his stated ethic, certainly; an infant in faith. Yet a Christian."[100] But Leithart also knows that this is not getting to the heart of the matter for Yoder; Leithart is aware that Yoder "is concerned not with Constantine the man but rather with the shift that Constantine symbolizes."[101] But, Leithart argues, this theological interest does not mean that Yoder can get away with reading his sources on the Constantinian shift in an incorrect manner. Yoder is making specific historical claims regarding the history of the church, and his mistakes contribute to distortions regarding his concept of "Constantinianism."[102]

Leithart points out that Yoder gets Eusebius wrong, as Yoder does not realize Eusebius was a theologian, who was driven by a theological project

---

Alexandria, Origin, Justin Martyr and Cyprian of Carthage do witness to how there existed in the early church an "ecosystem of peace," which disappeared in the centuries after Constantine. See Kreider, "'Converted' but Not Baptized," 30–31.

98. Leithart in his bibliography lists fourteen entries by Timothy Barnes and five entries by Hal Drake.

99. Alex Sider, in his doctoral dissertation on history and ecclesiology in Yoder's works, thus accounts for Yoder's sources on the Constantinian shift: "Yoder relied on the following texts, all of which are summational in character and reliant on nineteenth-century historiography: Bainton, *Christian Attitudes to War and Peace* (1960); Cadoux, *The Early Church and the World* (1925); Holmes, *War and Christian Ethics* (1975); Marrin, *War and the Christian Conscience* (1971)." See Sider, *To See History Doxologically*, 102.

100. Leithart, *Defending Constantine*, 96.

101. Leithart, *Defending Constantine*, 177.

102. Leithart, *Defending Constantine*, 178.

and Eusebius thus did not just replace Christ with the emperor and the church with the empire.[103] Leithart argues the understanding Yoder has of Eusebius comes from ignoring his larger apologetic and biblical authorship, and relying too narrowly on a bad reading of the *Vita Constantini*. To prove how carelessly Yoder reads the *Vita Constantini*, Leithart points out how Eusebius describes Constantine as a "sort of bishop," the quasi here being as important as the term "bishop," since it was Eusebius's attempt to reduce Constantine's role in the church.[104] According to Leithart, the use of this term worked to close off the more radical conception, according to which the emperor's office became identified with the office of a bishop, as it was about to happen under Constantine's son Constantius's reign, during which the *Vita Constantini* was written.[105] What for Yoder seems like Eusebius collapsing ecclesiastical and secular office, was, in reality, Eusebius attempting to protect the church from too large a secular influence. According to Leithart, Yoder's careless reading of Eusebius thereby led him to understand Eusebius saying the exact opposite of what he actually wanted to achieve.

Leithart does admit that Eusebius, especially in the *Vita Constantini*, interprets Constantine's rise to power in an overly enthusiastic manner. But Yoder failed to take into account, Leithart claims, how this drastic change must have felt for Christians in the fourth century:

> I have not found in Yoder a single word of gratitude to Constantine for keeping Roman officials from killing Christians for being Christians. I have not found a single word that shows any effort to get under the 'psychic skin' of bishops (like Eusebius) who witnessed Christians being roasted alive and then witnessed Constantine kissing the empty eye-sockets of a persecuted brother. Yoder shows little sign of trying to understand why the bishops answered the question 'Where should the emperor sit in council?' the way they did.[106]

With the help of explicit graphic detail Leithart makes the point that Yoder did not read Eusebius on his own terms. Yoder is drawing conclusions

---

103. Leithart, *Defending Constantine*, 179.

104. Leithart does not provide the Greek terms employed by Eusebius, but he does provide a reference to the English translation of Gilbert Dagron's *Empereur et prêtre*. The concept of a "sort of" universal bishop Leithart references can in Dagron's book be traced back to the expression οἷά τις κοινὸς ἐπίσκοπος in *VC* I:44.1, where Eusebius describes Constantine at the Council. See Dagron, *Emperor and Priest*, 133.

105. Leithart, *Defending Constantine*, 180.

106. Leithart, *Defending Constantine*, 182.

that are based rather on his preconceived Anabaptist ideas of the church than on a careful reading of Eusebius and his context.

If Yoder was unnuanced in his reading of Eusebius, it was nothing compared to his reading of Augustine. Leithart makes clear that Augustine wrote *De Civitate Dei* exactly as an antidote to Eusebianism.[107] On two areas Yoder misreads Augustine, the first being on the question of eschatology. According to Leithart's reading of Yoder, Augustine is not given enough credit for his eschatological theology. When Yoder says that Augustine believed the time leading up to the Constantinian shift was a time of progress culminating with Constantine, Leithart claims he has simply not read Augustine properly.[108]

The second of Yoder's misreadings of Augustine has to do with how Yoder believes Augustine merged the moral of the church with the moral of wider society. Leithart believes that Yoder's suggestion that Augustine "celebrates" the way things are is simply baffling. *De Civitate Dei*, Leithart assures, is exactly about distinguishing the shallow peace on this temporal earth from the genuine *shalom* of the kingdom.[109] Leithart believes that, for Augustine, Constantine was not "the hinge of the ages," and he quotes Robert Markus in that for Augustine "the Christianization of the Roman Empire is as accidental to the history of salvation as it is reversible."[110] With a classical Augustinian reference Leithart polemically concludes that "Yoder's Augustine is so far from the real Augustine that it is difficult to find a response beyond pointing to a copy of *City of God* with the exhortation *Tolle lege*."[111] The findings of the analysis of the *Vita Constantini* and the *De Civitate Dei* in part 2 and part 3 of this book showed Eusebius not to be a mere sycophant and Augustine to be critical toward Eusebius's interpretation of the Constantinian shift. These findings support Leithart's critique of Yoder's reading of Eusebius and Augustine.

It can be concluded that Leithart's criticism of Yoder's understanding of both Eusebius and Augustine is appropriate. We have now established that Yoder has a poor historical grasp on two areas vital for his interpretation of the Constantinian shift; both in regard to his understanding of pacifism in the early church and in regard to his understanding of Eusebius's

---

107. Leithart, *Defending Constantine*, 180.
108. Leithart, *Defending Constantine*, 285.
109. Leithart, *Defending Constantine*, 286.
110. Leithart, *Defending Constantine*, 286
111. Leithart, *Defending Constantine*, 286.

and Augustine's interpretation of the Constantinian shift. Leithart believes that "if he [Yoder] got Christian history wrong, that sets a question mark over his theology."[112]

In the following I will investigate whether and how Yoder's historical misreadings relate to the theological conclusions Yoder is drawing regarding the Constantinian shift.

4.3.2 Criticism of Yoder's Theological Analysis

Throughout the book we have seen how history and theology is related. When Yoder gets history wrong, it will cause theological trouble too. How Yoder's historical analysis influences his theology is what I will first look at here. Afterwards I will examine what Yoder's historical misunderstandings mean for the theological validity of his interpretation of the Constantinian shift.

Leithart believes that Yoder cannot know as much as he claims about the pacifist consensus of the early church, and he believes Yoder misreads Eusebius and especially Augustine. This together leads Yoder to an oversimplification of the history of mainstream Christianity to the point of caricature.[113] Leithart argues that such a misrepresentation results in two grave problems for Yoder's theological program. The first problem is that his poor grasp of history undermines Yoder's whole idea of a Constantinian shift. Yoder's idea of an abrupt Constantinian shift, in terms of a changed ethic and life of the church, simply cannot be established if one reads the sources carefully: "If 'Constantinian' is taken to mean a 'merger' of church and empire in which the Christians identify some nation or empire or ruler with the movement of God in history, there was a brief, ambiguous 'Constantinian moment' in the early fourth century, and there have been many tragic 'Constantinian moments' since. There was no permanent, epochal 'Constantinian shift.'"[114] Leithart does not deny that Constantine's rise led to a change in the life of the church, and that the new context the church found itself in naturally did lead to a new understanding of its place in the world. But he believes that Yoder's flawed historical scholarship led to a misconstruction of how it happened historically and, most importantly, led to an unwarranted condemnation of the theology that took responsibility

---

112. Leithart, *Defending Constantine*, 154.
113. Leithart, *Defending Constantine*, 305.
114. Leithart, *Defending Constantine*, 287.

for society; a theology that Leithart believes was one of the positive outcomes of a church moving closer to the rulers of the empire.

According to Leithart, Yoder failed to appreciate what Constantine actually achieved. Yoder's lack of understanding of the situation of the church around the time of Constantine came to mean that Yoder could not properly appreciate what Constantinianism has actually contributed with in a positive sense for the church. Leithart points out that if, in contemporary North America, a session of the Senate opened with religious sacrifice, talk radio would be abuzz for months and there would be marches in the streets.[115] Yoder's one-sided critique of Constantinianism did not allow him to see how a state protecting the church has benefitted the church in ways that are hard to imagine being any different today.

Yoder's view of history was "monological" in that just one narrative came to dominate his whole interpretation of history.[116] He interpreted the development of the Western church only in the light of the Constantinian shift as a decline; he did not question this narrative, and therefore did not account properly for the multiple aspects of the development of the relationship between church and state throughout Western history.[117] This flawed methodology led Yoder to draw unwarranted theological consequences.

---

115. Leithart, *Defending Constantine*, 329.

116. Sider, *To See History Doxologically*, 103.

117. Also a characteristic of Eusebius's interpretation of the Constantinian shift was a single narrative guiding the interpretation of the Constantinian shift, and thereby missing the equivocal nature of historical events, seldom to be understood in just one way. Hal Drake has argued that Eusebius operates with a "totalizing discourse"; i.e., an explanatory mode, where one answer fits all. See Drake, *Constantine and the Bishops*, 360. The possibility persists that Eusebius's one-sided interpretation of the Constantinian shift was related to his Arian leanings. One could venture the guess that Yoder's "monological" interpretation of the Constantinian shift also can be traced back to a non-trinitarian mindset. Within the plural strands of the early Radical Reformation, there were a number of theologians denying the Trinity and instead championing a Christology of subordination. Adam Pastor, an early Mennonite leader who was later expelled, can serve as an example. See Templin, "Adam Pastor: Anti-Trinitarian Anabaptist," 29. It is a possibility that a monological interpretation of history is a trait found in the works of theologians sharing a Christology of subordination, and in Yoder's interpretation of the Constantinian shift we do see structures from early tenets of Radical Reformation theology tacitly setting themselves through. That the influence from a non-trinitarian mindset should be what led both Eusebius and Yoder to interpret history in a "monological" manner, will remain a guess and two arguments count against it. First, Yoder was influenced from multiple sources and he often emphasized the importance of the dogma of the Trinity. Second, such direct congruence between a theologians trinitarian or non-trinitarian views and his or her interpretation of history, though an enticing idea, is hard to prove.

Leithart's critique is appropriate in regard to Yoder's historical scholarship, but does Leithart's critique also mean that Yoder's interpretation of the Constantinian shift can be categorized as wrong? I am not sure.

On the last two pages of *Defending Constantine* Leithart recapitulates his theological critique of Yoder:

> He failed, as Augustine said against Pelagius, to give due weight to "the interim, the interval between the remission of sins which takes place in baptism, and the permanently established sinless state in the kingdom that is to come, this middle time [tempus hoc medium] of prayer, while [we] must pray, 'Forgive us our sins.'" He failed to acknowledge that all—Constantine, Rome, ourselves—stand in medial time, and yet are no less Christian for that.[118]

That is a strong criticism of Yoder by way of Augustine's criticism of Pelagius. But it is also a misreading of Yoder's interpretation of the Constantinian shift. Yoder's problem with the Constantinian shift is not that Christians "stand in medial time," and did not manage to live perfect virtuous lives. Yoder was aware that the church will always fail and cannot be perfect in the here and now. As we saw above, Yoder's interpretation and critique of the Constantinian shift was instead focused on what he believed was the church having forgotten which theological authorities properly ought to guide it. The problem instituted by the Constantinian shift was that the church began to see the ethic of the church guided by the moral common sense of wider society and that it forgot who is in control of history. Yoder's critique was not that the church did not live up to its ideals, but rather that it had forgotten them.

The critique of Yoder's historical scholarship did prove that Yoder could not connect his critique of the Constantinian shift to historical events quite the way he did. But does that mean Yoder is mistaken in his larger interpretation of the Constantinian shift and what it led to in respect to changes in mentality? Grand questions touching on the relationship between theology and history, which I will move closer to in the conclusion.

Leithart himself acknowledges that the historical criticism might not get to the core of Yoder's theological project, and the last chapter of *Defending Constantine* is therefore a long venture into disproving Yoder's ideas about pacifism and about the relationship between church and state

---

118. Leithart, *Defending Constantine*, 341–42. The additions to Augustine's text in square brackets are inserted by Leithart.

on grounds of Scripture and tradition.[119] Though agreeing to some of the criticism Yoder raised in regard to the Constantinian shift, Leithart's theological starting point is markedly different, and Leithart has his own theological program. What this consists of will not be further explored here, but the outline of it, as Jonathan Tran has also identified, centers around how, on the basis of Scripture and tradition, Leithart wants to prove that ecclesiastical entanglement between church and state power does not need to be accommodationist.[120]

But how and to what extent can the church be entangled with the state power without it leading to the church forgetting its commission? Is the church to live in harmony and in support of the surrounding society, or is it to stand out as an alternative and thereby witness to the world? As I will lay out in the next section, the view on that question seems to be one of the determinative factors for the interpretation of the Constantinian shift.

4.4 Yoder and the Ancient Interpretations

Mennonite theologian Thomas Finger in 1994 published an article in which he identified the (maybe unexpected) similarities between Anabaptism and Eastern Orthodoxy.[121] In this section, I will use what Finger identified as the three points of theological agreement between Anabaptist theology and Orthodox theology to provide a structure for the comparison of the theological underpinning of the interpretations of the Constantinian shift.

Finger mentions how it could seem odd that Eastern Orthodox theology and Anabaptist theology would share traits, as the one has a long history with an elaborate sacramental and liturgical life and the other consists of small informal churches springing from what has often been identified as the left wing of the Reformation.[122] Despite these differences, Finger points out three similarities and one strong dissimilarity between the theologies of the two church communities. Similarity is found on: (a) The concept of the church as a visible witness and manifestation of humanity's transcendent

---

119. Leithart, *Defending Constantine*, 301–42.
120. Tran, "*Defending Constantine* Taken Seriously," 129.
121. Finger, "Anabaptism and Eastern Orthodoxy."
122. Finger, "Anabaptism and Eastern Orthodoxy," 67–68. Ernst Troeltsch initiated a line of historical interpretation, according to which the Anabaptist churches were regarded as forerunners of the modern secular worldview, which the Orthodox Church so strongly critiques. See Finger, "Anabaptism and Eastern Orthodoxy," 69–70.

destiny (related to the question of how the (in)visible church is to be in the world). (b) Redemption understood as divinization (related to the question of the church and war).[123] (c) A concept of the eschatological inbreaking of God's reign (related to the question of the church and eschatology). But, as a very important point, (d) Finger identifies how Anabaptist and Orthodox theology strongly disagree on the church-world relationship.[124]

Below a short overview of where Eusebius, Augustine and Yoder fall in regard to these four tenets, and then in the rest of the section I will examine in detail the first three similarities, as they align with questions to have surfaced through this book. As the interpretations of Eusebius and Augustine has already been compared, I will here compare Yoder's interpretation of the Constantinian shift to that of the ancient bishops.

The analysis of Eusebius's and Yoder's interpretations of the Constantinian shift does support Finger's findings in terms of what Orthodox and Anabaptist theology would agree on.[125] (a) We saw that both Eusebius and Yoder in their interpretations of the Constantinian shift had a similar vision of the visible church as the true church. (b) Eusebius and Yoder were both focused on the divinization or sanctification of Christians, which would result in a different way of life. (c) For both Eusebius's and Yoder's interpretation of the Constantinian shift, the inbreaking of God's reign in the world played a role. (d) Yet Eusebius and Yoder disagreed on the key question of how to perceive the relationship between the church and the empire/state.

---

123. Divinization (*theosis*) is a highly developed theological concept within orthodox theology but bears a strong similarity to how Anabaptists understood grace. Despite their origin around the time of the Reformation, Anabaptists often have a theology of grace quite different from the Magisterial Reformers. Whereas grace for the Magisterial Reformers was conceived as largely forensic ("as God's declaration of acceptance and pardon. Thus, they interpreted any preoccupation with behavior as human efforts to gain salvation"), grace was by Anabaptists conceived as "a transforming divine energy." See Finger, "Anabaptism and Eastern Orthodoxy," 76.

124. Finger, "Anabaptism and Eastern Orthodoxy," 67. Aside from these three points of agreement and one point of disagreement, Finger also lists "theocentric anthropology" as a point of similarity between Anabaptist and Orthodox theology. See Finger, "Anabaptism and Eastern Orthodoxy," 83–86. Questions pertaining to theological anthropology have not had a prominent place in the examined interpretations of the Constantinian shift, and, except from how it overlaps with questions of divinization, will not be pursued as an area for comparison here.

125. Eusebius cannot be said to be a direct representative of the Eastern Orthodox Church, but the Orthodox Church does attempt to remain close to this early theology and does derive its theology from sources like Eusebius. As Finger's article addresses some of the core beliefs, it can thereby work as a framework for analyzing both ancient and contemporary texts.

If we utilize the above categories to compare the theological underpinnings of Yoder's and Augustine's interpretation of the Constantinian shift, we see a different pattern emerge. If Yoder shared theological tenet 1-3 with Eusebius, he shared instead the fourth with Augustine. (a) Augustine did not hold the visible church to be identical with the true church. For him, this relationship between the visible and the true church is more subtle, as the true church is spiritual and not immediately identical with the institutional church. (b) Augustine did not emphasize the divinization or sanctification of the Christian. (c) The Constantinian shift was not interpreted as the direct inbreaking of God's reign or as an apostasy from Christ's commission to the church. (d) But Augustine came significantly closer to Yoder in the question of the church-world relationship.

4.4.1 The Church in the World

Now I will look further into the first point: how their understanding of the (in)visibility of the true church came to structure the three interpretations of the Constantinian shift. For both Yoder and Eusebius no strong distinction is made between the true church and the visible, institutional church. Eusebius did operate with a distinction between the internal and the external affairs of the church, but he did not in the *VC* draw a distinction between the institution of the church and the true church. Yoder made it an explicit point of his to argue that the idea of the invisible church was faulty. To be aware that Eusebius and Yoder shared the perception of the visible church as the true church makes it palpable how they perceived very differently the role of the church in the world. When the church was faring better politically it prompted Eusebius to give a positive theological evaluation of the Constantinian shift. Likewise, when Yoder saw that the church was not living up to its "political" commitment, it prompted him to give a negative theological evaluation of the Constantinian shift.[126] They agreed on the visibility of the church, but strongly disagreed on how the church ought to relate to wider society. This pattern in their interpretations of the Constantinian shift is congruent with Finger's analysis, as Eusebius's and Yoder's different interpretations of the Constantinian shift reveal their

---

126. As mentioned earlier, Yoder did not use the term "political" in a conventional sense, in terms of engaging in the political game but rather in the meaning of the church's way of life in the world; itself being a political witness to how to live and order communal life differently.

theological presuppositions. That Anabaptist and Orthodox theology disagree on the key question of the relationship between the church and the world makes it comprehensible how Eusebius and Yoder at the same time could hold similar views on significant theological dogmas (point 1-3) but reach vastly different interpretations of the Constantinian shift.[127]

Like Yoder, Augustine was also highly critical of a church forgetting to whom it owed its loyalty. It could be assumed that would lead to a similar ecclesiology between Yoder and Augustine. But that is not the case, as they hold very different notions of the church. To better understand the relationship between Yoder and Augustine, I need to take a small detour into contemporary scholarship on Yoder. Augustine interpreted the Constantinian shift not immediately in terms of progress nor decline, but rather as a ripple on the surface of God's grand plan for the world. Unfortunately, Yoder was not aware of how close Augustine's interpretation of the Constantinian shift was to his own interpretation. As we saw above, Yoder held the view that Augustine's theology was vastly different from his own and believed that Augustine wanted an internalized invisible Christianity, whereas Yoder saw himself as the proponent of a visible church, which followed the example of Christ. But Yoder is exaggerating the difference.

In his dissertation, "A Nonviolent Augustinianism? History and Politics in the Theologies of St. Augustine and John Howard Yoder," Charles Mayo Collier demonstrates that had Yoder been a better reader of Augustine, he would have saved himself some trouble. Collier points out how Augustine and Yoder are often contrasted due to their differing views on violence, but he suggests that Augustine's and Yoder's "theopolitical visions"

---

127. Contemporary Orthodox theologian Vigen Guroian recognizes that the early church may have overly embraced the benefits of uniting the church with the secular powers, since it led the church to forget "two fundamental perceptions about its relation to the world and its mission in the world. First, in its efforts to sanctify the social order, the Church forgot its earlier experience of the world both as created good and as a fallen, mortally sick order. The Church, having said *yes* to the invitation to render the empire holy before God, forgot how to say *no* to the imperial claims that Byzantium was the Kingdom of God already realized on earth. Second, the Church permitted itself to be defined as a hierarchy, with the *authority* of spiritual dogmas and the *power* of sacramental graces, at the terrible price of losing sight of its calling as a *free community of faith*, whose very presence in the world is to be both a judgment and a limitation upon the claims of all worldly authorities and powers to being ends in themselves." See Guroian, *Incarnate Love*, 123. Such an evaluation of the Constantinian shift and what followed from it qualifies as a strong revision of Eusebius's interpretation, and serves as an example of how the Constantinian shift can be interpreted by (slightly dissenting) Orthodox theology in a manner significantly closer to Yoder's interpretation.

can be said to be aligned in regard to how the church's being in the world in itself constitutes another politics.[128] Collier points out that Augustine's Christianity was not only about internalization: "What Augustine does so dramatically in the *City of God* is contest the surface meanings of history, including the 'triumph' of Christianity that came with the baptism of Constantine. Moreover, the Augustine who repeatedly turns inward in the Confessions is the same Augustine who refuses Eusebian readings of Christian empire in the City of God."[129] Both Augustine and Yoder saw the church as a community in exile, and they both ended up using the Babylonian exile as the metaphor for the role of the church in the world.[130] The question that Augustine left hanging, Gerald Schlabach argues, is how the pilgrim community is to live in the world? But with his message of peacemaking Yoder answered this question.[131]

Augustine and Yoder agreed on a critical stance toward a church forgetting who it owed its primary loyalty, and yet, unlike Yoder, Augustine did not prescribe how this would look for the life and thought of the church. On that point Yoder had a concept of a visible church, which was quite different from Augustine's theology on the true invisible church.

Augustine and Yoder were both critical toward Eusebius's interpretation of the Constantinian shift, but their theological presuppositions in regard to the political and visible nature of the church were so divergent that they came to interpret the Constantinian shift differently. For Augustine it was a ripple on the surface of God's grand plan, whereas for Yoder it meant a fatal decline of the church.

We have now seen how Thomas Finger's first point of similarity between Orthodox and Anabaptist theology (the church perceived as a visible manifestation) came to be important for the interpretation of the church in relation to the state. Finger's second identified point of similarity; regarding the question of divinization, was important for how the three theologians thought about the church and war.

128. Collier, "Nonviolent Augustinianism?," iv.

129. Collier, "Nonviolent Augustinianism?," 90.

130. Schlabach, "Christian Witness in the Earthly City." Martin Luther also extensively used the metaphor of the Babylonian captivity but interestingly not in the manner of Augustine and Yoder to describe the relationship between church and world. Luther instead transposed the metaphor to depict the Catholic Church as the kingdom of Babylon: "weiß ich jetzt und bin gewiß, dass das Papsttum das babylonische Reich . . . ist." See Luther, *Von der babylonischen Gefangenschaft der Kirche*, 172.

131. Schlabach, "Christian Witness in the Earthly City."

4.4.2 The Church and War

The different estimations of war and violence were significant in the examined interpretations of the Constantinian shift. The issue of war stresses whether the church ought to support or to critique the actions of the state, and thus the three theologians have different evaluations of this question. Eusebius lauds how victorious Constantine was in battles, though he occasionally acknowledges the evil nature of wars.[132] Augustine holds war to be sinful and believes it has to be curtailed in the best possible way—the concept of just war is, for him, a way to achieve this. Yoder believes engaging in war is not following the example of Christ, and therefore cannot be supported by the church or be the course of action to take by a Christian.

These three views on war is related to underlying theological ways of thinking about the church in the world and of thinking about sin. Again, with the caveat that Eusebius cannot be said to be a representative for the contemporary Orthodox Church, Orthodox and Anabaptist theological similarity in regard to their concept of divinization manifests itself in Eusebius's and Yoder's interpretation of the Constantinian shift and war. Though Eusebius and Yoder held opposite views on the church's role in regard to war, they shared the notion that war is a question of deep interest for the church. Eusebius believed that war could be God's way of bringing into effect God's will in the world, and he therefore depicted Constantine as the successful warlord, who realized God's plan in the world, and obviously the church was to be supportive of this endeavor, according to Eusebius. Yoder shared Eusebius's notion of the church as a "political" entity, and he also believed the question of war was an issue the church ought to be invested in, though Yoder envisioned the role of the church in relation to war in a quite different manner than Eusebius. For Yoder, the church is carrying out the will of God not by supporting war but rather by opposing it. Despite their different estimations of war, they shared the idea that the question of war was a matter highly relevant for the church. Additionally, they both maintained that the corruption of sin did not hinder Christians in carrying out the will of God.

Yoder and Augustine, too, differed on their views of war and how the church should relate to it. Augustine acknowledged that war is a great evil but also believed that it is part of the order of this fallen world, and

---

132. That Eusebius depicted Constantine as victorious in battles might not be an expression of theological concern but rather motivated by his desire to give a favorable portrayal of Constantine. Nevertheless, a certain theology of war is still expressed.

developed what later was to become a theory for how the state could go about handling war in the best way. Yoder believed that the church lives by a narrative different than the one characterizing this fallen world, and he developed a theology for not how the state ought to relate to war but for how the church was to relate to war. Put sharply Augustine held that sin is pervasive, and the church needs to be realistic about this—Yoder held that grace is what defines the church and it therefore partakes in another story.

I just used the word "realistic" to describe Augustine's approach to the question of war. Such a description brings to mind the adjectives often applied to Reinhold Niebuhr's view of politics and war. To equate Augustine and Reinhold Niebuhr would be an anachronistic mistake, but it is fair to say that the Lutheran Reinhold Niebuhr's view of sin was not far removed from that of Augustine. A focus on the relationship between the theology of Yoder and Niebuhr can be a way to shed light on how the different estimations of the power of sin led them to interpret differently the Constantinian shift. Yoder characterized Reinhold Niebuhr's view on sin thus: "Niebuhr said: 'no; sin is not only our situation, it is also our nature.'"[133] According to such an understanding of the human condition, any attempt to contest war as a dominating societal order would obviously fall out unsuccessful. But Yoder does not share such a view on sin. In a collection of essays honoring Yoder, Gerald Schlabach points out that "we begin parting with Niebuhr when we insist that divine grace is empowering, not just merciful—transforming, not just forgiving."[134] This disagreement between Yoder and Niebuhr goes to the core of Augustine's and Yoder's disagreement on how to conceive of sin and grace. From Yoder's perspective, grace is understood as playing a transformative role, and it therefore becomes plausible for him that Christians in community can act in ways that would sustain a pacifist way of life.

To be aware of this theologically different underpinning pertaining to the question of sin and grace helps to clarify how Augustine and Yoder reached different views on the question of war, which the Constantinian shift made such a pertinent question.

---

133. Yoder, *Christian Attitudes to War, Peace, and Revolution*, 344.
134. Schlabach, "Deuteronomic or Constantinian," 455.

4.4.3 The Church and Eschatology

Finger identified as a third point of similarity in beliefs between Orthodox and Anabaptist theology the idea of the eschatological inbreaking of God's reign. This similarity becomes visible in Eusebius's and Yoder's interpretation of the Constantinian shift. Both Yoder and Eusebius interpreted the Constantinian shift in terms of a development. For Eusebius, the Constantinian shift is considered to be a realization of God's plan, and the eschatological inbreaking thereby takes place in an identifiable manner with the Constantinian shift. We saw that for Yoder, the place to identify God's activity in the world is not in "secular" history but predominantly in the life and witness of the church, and Yoder interpreted the Constantinian shift as a decline. Eusebius and Yoder perceived differently how to recognize God's reign breaking into the world and they disagreed as to what it looked like, but they both maintained that it could be identified—either in the activity of the empire or in the activity of the church.

Augustine conceived of the question of God's reign breaking into the world differently. He did not hold it to be possible to identify God's acts in the world outside of the *historia sacra*. Neither in the political history of the world nor in the story of the church were God's acts in the world clearly to be identified. Yoder did not share Augustine's disconnect between the true church and the visible church, and Yoder did believe that it was possible to point to the church as the place, where God's reign (sometimes) becomes visible in the world. The pattern again emerges that Eusebius and Yoder agree structurally (that God's reign breaking into the world can be identified), but they disagree as to where this is to be identified; whereas Augustine disagrees with both of them by pointing to that God's reign cannot be identified in this world outside of the *historia sacra*.

How a theologian thinks regarding one dogma often influences how that theologian conceives of other aspects of theology too—when one end of a lever goes down the other end comes up. The dogmas of eschatology and creation are strongly interdependent. The notion a theologian holds regarding the ultimate purpose of the church and the world often reveals something about how that theologian estimates creation.[135] Also in the

---

135. An emblematic example of this principle is to be found in the theology of Irenaeus. For Irenaeus creation was imperfect, it did not arrive in full bloom, but had to mature in order to receive its full perfection in Christ by the end of time. Thus, how Irenaeus perceived of eschatology was strongly interdependent with his theology of creation. See Bretherton, *Christianity and Contemporary Politics*, 196.

work of the theologians analyzed in this book such ab internal connection in their thinking reveals itself.

Eusebius interprets the Constantinian shift in a manner that holds wider society in high regard. For him, the church is contributing to the common good of society, and Eusebius does not think of the church in opposition to wider society, at least not after Constantine's arrival. According to Eusebius, God's reign is breaking through when Constantine gets to rule the empire. Yoder interprets the Constantinian shift differently. For Yoder, God's reign breaks in not through the secular state but through the church.[136] Yoder does not think the church shall not contribute to the common good of society, but he believes the right way for the church to do so is by living as if the story of God is true and thereby be a witness for the rest of creation. Yoder likewise does not hold God to be primarily active through creation but rather through the church.[137]

Pertaining to how to evaluate creation and the common good, the theological model Augustine presents is a corrective to both Eusebius and Yoder. As we saw, the question of how to interpret the "secular" common good in Augustine's writing can be a contested question. Augustine believes that the church can contribute to the common good, but he also holds that the true church is really only a pilgrim people who does not belong to this world. In that sense Augustine, at the same time, holds that the created world is good and important, but also very temporary. In the same way as Augustine views the Constantinian shift as a ripple on the surface of history, he understands all of creation as something that is only a temporary place for the true pilgrim church.

4.5 Conclusion

A general pattern emerged throughout the comparison of the theological underpinnings of the three interpretations of the Constantinian shift. Eusebius and Yoder shared theological views (a) on how to perceive the church

---

136. Yoder argues that with the Constantinian shift the misunderstanding came about that "the true meaning of history, the true locus of salvation, is in the cosmos and not in the church. What God is really doing is being done primarily through the framework of society as a whole and not in the Christian community." See Yoder, *Royal Priesthood*, 198.

137. It is a misnomer on the basis of this view to accuse Yoder of being sectarian. But for him the contribution of the church to the common temporal good of society is first and foremost in the form of a witness of Christ.

as visible, (b) on the deification of human beings and (c) on how to perceive of the inbreaking of God's reign in the world. But they differed on the fourth key question of how to conceive of the relationship between church and world. Augustine stood closer to Yoder than Eusebius on the question of how to understand the relationship between church and world, but Augustine disagreed with both Eusebius and Yoder in regard to the other three theological areas. That explains how Yoder and Eusebius in their interpretation of the Constantinian shift could agree on many central aspects of how to conceive of the church as a visible "political" entity, but still arrive at very different evaluations of the Constantinian shift. Whereas Augustine and Yoder to a large extent shared theological views on how the church is to relate to the empire/state but disagreed on the three other areas.

We saw that contemporary scholarship has pointed out how Yoder's theology is closer to Augustine's theology than Yoder himself was aware. This book supports such a conclusion, but also nuances the picture by pointing out how Yoder's interpretation of the Constantinian shift reveals many structural similarities to Eusebius's theology. In terms of how the church ought to relate to the state Yoder was closest to Augustine, but on the emphasis of the "political" nature of the church, Yoder stood closest to Eusebius.

These questions encompass the contentions in Eusebius's, Augustine's, and Yoder's interpretations of the Constantinian shift, but can, at the same time, be said to touch on subjects pertaining to central tenants of trinitarian theology: the church in the world pertains to God as the creator of church and world; the church and war, in sense of war as the most vivid expression of sin, pertains to Christ as the redeemer of sin; the question of the church and eschatology pertains to the Holy Spirit as the sustainer of the church in the world. An analysis of Eusebius's, Augustine's and Yoder's interpretations of the Constantinian shift has thus provided insights into central areas of their theological thinking.

As mentioned in the introduction, what led Eusebius, Augustine, and Yoder to interpret the Constantinian shift the way they did was not only theological reasoning; social, political, economic etc. factors have exerted influence too. However, these historical contexts have been accounted for and summed up throughout the book.

The focus of this book has been the theological underpinnings of the three interpretations of the Constantinian shift. To display the theological connection between their interpretation of the Constantinian shift and what theological underpinning sustained such interpretations helps to understand why Eusebius, Augustine, and Yoder interpreted the same historical event so diversely. Furthermore, an understanding of what is at stake theologically contributes to a better understanding of the theological aspects in the question of the relationship between the church and the state. An awareness of the theological underpinnings of these paradigmatic interpretations of the Constantinian shift helps to understand why the events of the fourth century could be accounted for so differently through the history of the church. Hereby the historical investigation is brought to a conclusion.

The existence of such three rather diverse theological interpretations of the Constantinian shift can be taken as evidence that the church also after the council of Nicaea continued to care about the dogmatic differences, which Constantine mentioned in his letter to Arius and Alexander. These "very silly questions," even though overlooking them might lead to fewer quarrels, continues to be important for the church; and the ultimate goal of the state (defined as creating a harmonious society?) and the ultimate goal of the church (defined as a truthful witness of the Christian gospel?) does not always align as elegantly as Eusebius depicted it.

This book has given an insight into how the historiography of the Constantinian shift is informed by theological underpinnings related to larger theological questions of the relationship between church and world, and it has pointed to foundational questions of the relationship between theology and history-writing. For a short deliberation of what can be taken away from all this we will turn to the last part of the book.

PART V:

Perspectives

5

Church, History and Theology

AT THE CORE OF how to interpret the Constantinian shift lies the question of how to be the church in the world but not of the world. To directly address that question is not the aim of this book, as the answer will always be inseparable from the context of the specific congregation. However, three different models of how the church is to be positioned in the world are integral to the three interpretations of the Constantinian shift investigated. I will in the first section of part 5 attempt to tease out these three models, as they help to give a fuller picture of what prompted Eusebius, Augustine and Yoder to interpret the Constantinian shift so differently and, at the same time, offer insights that prove helpful for how to think about church and state relations in contemporary society.

Throughout the book, the question of the relationship between a theological account and a historical account has continually emerged. We saw that due to the nature of the gospel, theology is bound to deal with historical accounts. Likewise, historical writing, in narrating the past and explaining past political events, easily falls into using theologically loaded language. A short deliberation on the validity of theological history-writing will make up the second section of part 5.

In the third and last section of these perspectives I will look at the position of ecclesiology in the Western theological tradition. The changes that took place with the Constantinian shift can help to explain why the church was never given a major independent place in Western theology. The changes that the role of the church in the West is currently undergoing herald new possibilities for theology and for the church.

5.1 Three Interpretations of the Place of the Church in the World

A specific vision of how the church is to be in the world is inherent to each interpretation of the Constantinian shift.

Eusebius envisioned the church as aligned with the world. The church and the world were not to be conflated, according to Eusebius. Nevertheless, with the ascent of Constantine, God had finally directed the course of history to a point where the church and the Roman Empire had similar concerns and could pursue harmonious interests, Eusebius believed. That meant that Eusebius did not believe that the church should be critical toward the Roman Empire but, on the contrary, should work with the Empire toward the final culmination of God's plan. The eschatological expectancy was not strong for Eusebius, in the sense that, with the Constantinian shift, it was already the start of a new age, where the church would flourish. Eusebius's vision is a church that is closely aligned to the world, as, in a way, the eschatological reality has already begun with Constantine.[1]

Augustine had a somewhat different vision. For him the church is peregrinating in the world. The Constantinian shift was not interpreted as a progression but rather as a ripple on the surface of history. It did not herald any fundamental changes to the condition of the church in the world. According to his model, the church is indeed distinct from the world. However, Augustine's theological move, toward perceiving an invisible church as the real church, removed the visible political expression. When, at some point, the eschatological realization would be fulfilled, all creation would perish while the true members of the church would get a new perfect

---

1. To venture a comparison across centuries—Eusebius's view of history brings to mind the 1992 book *The End of History and the Last Man* by American political scientist Francis Fukuyama, see *The End of History and the Last Man*. Fukuyama claimed that history had reached its culmination with the fall of the Berlin Wall, and that liberal democracy would now, slowly but victoriously, march through the world. In the same way as Eusebius was not quite right that a new epoch of Christian peace would ensue after Constantine, Fukuyama's prediction did not hold up so straightforwardly. Nevertheless, such a similarity between Eusebius and Fukuyama ought not, maybe, to come as a surprise. Fukuyama's view of history was influenced by G. W. F. Hegel (1770–1831), who himself had been reading Eusebius in his student days, a fact which possibly affected Hegel's perception of the progressive nature of history, see Tassi, *Hegel a Berna: le premesse di un sistema*, 16.

body.² Augustine's vision for the church can be likened to an ark that travels through the world but will eventually be leaving the world behind.

Yoder combined elements from both models. In agreement with Augustine, Yoder believed the church to be a pilgrim in this world, distinctly different from the secular state. But, contrary to Augustine, for Yoder, the church was not conceived of as something invisible or "inner," but rather as a visible political reality. Like Eusebius, Yoder believed that God leads human beings to a different form of life. On the other hand, contrary to Eusebius, he did not believe that this would be realized through a change in wider society. For Yoder, the model of the church can be likened to a garden, where the gardener sows the flowers for the rest of the world to marvel at until the *eschaton*, at which point the rest of the world will be lifted up to become like the garden.³

5.2 The Validity of Theological History-Writing

Throughout the analysis of the three interpretations of the Constantinian shift it has become clear that their respective accounts of history had many theological features. That ought not to surprise anyone, though; taking into account the historical and political aspects of the gospel is not foreign for any constructive theology.

However, a question remains unanswered—how is the value of a historical account affected, when it is so clearly influenced by theological presuppositions? The question became specifically relevant for both Eusebius's and Yoder's accounts of history. They were driven by a theological vision, which to some extent blurred their historical vision.⁴ They were not predominantly preoccupied with the historical "truth," but rather with giving a theological account of history. Does that mean that they were not giving a true interpretation of the Constantinian shift? Obviously, that has to do with what a "true theological account of history" is considered to look like. Is an account of history supposed to describe what events occurred, or, rather, is it supposed to convey a theological vision? Such a question leads

2. *ciu.* XX:16.

3. For a beautiful unfolding of the garden as a metaphor for the church see Sider, *To See History Doxologically*, 9–11.

4. Yoder's focus on the pacifist nature of the early church serves as an example. It is still unclear, to what extent, exactly, the early church adhered to pacifist convictions, but there is little doubt that Yoder's theological presuppositions skew his perspective on the historical reality of the early church.

to more philosophical questions regarding the nature of a true historical account, which we will not entertain here.

I will, however, allow myself one brief excursus into New Testament studies, as the insights from recent debates in that field might help to cast light on the question of the validity of theological history-writing. Earlier on, we examined Leithart's criticism of Yoder's historical scholarship; but without reaching a conclusion as to whether identifying these faults meant that Yoder's interpretation of the Constantinian shift was not "true"? One of the insights offered by the New Perspective on Paul in New Testament studies concerned how to read Romans 7:19: "For I do not do the good I want, but the evil I do not want is what I do" (NRSV). E. P. Sanders, among others, has pointed out that Paul is talking about the condition before he became Christian, and not his condition as a Christian.[5] From Paul's perspective the statement is, in all probability, not meant to say something about the Christian predicament. Nevertheless, this was how Luther and Calvin understood it. They understood the verse to be the archetypical expression of the human condition. Moreover, their interpretation does resonate with the experience of Christian life in the sixteenth century and later Western Christianity's preoccupation with questions of guilt. Does the fact that Luther's and Calvin's understanding derives from an inaccurate reading of Paul make it a false statement on the conditions of being a Christian in the West? I do not think so. Luther's account adequately depicts a common experience. Likewise, I believe Yoder still expresses a valid theological point in his interpretation of the Constantinian shift, despite the fact that his historical scholarship, and the scholarship he relied on, was flawed.[6]

---

5. In Sanders's words: "But Rom. 7:14–25 is in itself an exaggeration, being part of a statement that those in the flesh are entirely unable to observe the law, while those in the Spirit keep it. Paul's passion there lends seriousness to the passage, and we may all perhaps be forgiven for thinking that it is a profound statement of the human condition. It is best seen, as we argued above, and as Heikki Räisänen has pointed out, as an exaggerated view of the non-Christian life which depends on Paul's view of life in the Spirit." See Sanders, *Paul, the Law, and the Jewish People*, 124. In his overview of the New Perspective Stephen Westerholm sums up the position more bombastically: "We will first consider whether Paul could have written 7:14–25 of his *Christian* experience (97–104). The answer must be an emphatic, No!" See Westerholm, *Israel's Law and the Church's Faith*, 60.

6. The following pertinent quotation makes it clear that Westerholm likewise believed one can still learn something from Luther regarding Paul, despite the corrections of the New Perspective: "Students who want to know how a Rabbinic Jew perceived humanity's place in God's world will read Paul with caution and Luther not at all. On the other hand, students who want to understand Paul, but feel that they have nothing to learn from a Martin Luther, should consider a career in metallurgy." See Westerholm, *Israel's*

Neither of the three interpretations of the Constantinian shift contributed an accurate historical account. They did, however, contribute three theological interpretations of the Constantinian shift, all of which fall somewhere between a historical and a theological account. These works need to be approached as the theological documents they rightly are. When they are read as such, their "use" of the historical event can actually provide insights into the "actual" historical events. More importantly, however, their account of a historical event like the Constantinian shift conveys a larger theological message regarding the character of the relationship between church and world.

5.3 A Way Forward for the Church

It can be argued that only within the last century the church as a subject in itself has gained a strong independent position on the theological agenda.[7] Hence, in contemporary theology an understanding has arisen that ecclesiology is an area, which needs to be given more attention. But how is it that this area of theology has not been properly developed? Ought not the doctrines unfold organically so that all areas are given their due attention?

At least two theological understandings of the development of doctrine can be identified: one, primarily found in Catholic theology, argues that a natural and logical unfolding of doctrine, which exists *in nucleus* in Scripture, has taken place throughout the history of the church.[8] Another, most significantly expressed in nineteenth-century critical protestant scholarship, holds the view that church doctrines have been formed in order to accommodate political, economic, societal etc. pressure. This is a critical view of the development of doctrine, which argues that there is no guarantee that Christian doctrine will unfold in a specific manner.

Law and the Church's Faith, 173. Theologians like Luther and Yoder, who are driven by a strong theological vision in their reading of texts, are not the best sources when it comes to understanding the text or the historical events "in themselves." However, in order to understand something about the God, about whom these texts witness, such theological readings are most insightful.

7. "It is only in the late-modern period and particularly in the post-World War II ecumenical movement that the church has become an explicit and systematically central object of theological reflection." See Jenson, "Church and the Sacraments," 207.

8. For the paradigmatic example of this view of doctrinal development, see Newman, *Essay on the Development of Christian Doctrine*, 94–204.

If we are to follow the first view, it is puzzling why ecclesiology has not been developed more strongly in the theological tradition. There is, first and foremost, an abundancy of biblical material (especially in the writings of Paul), which could have led to the development of a strong doctrinal foundation for ecclesiology in connection with, second, a relationship between pneumatology and ecclesiology, which could have led to the development of a stronger independent locus for ecclesiology rooted in trinitarian thinking. If, on the other hand, we apply insights from the second view on doctrinal development, we see that external factors affect how church doctrines develop, also in relation to ecclesiology. I would posit the theory that the Constantinian shift was one such external factor which led to an array of Church doctrines remaining underdeveloped.

Throughout this book we have seen that there is an inherent doctrinal connection between ecclesiology, sanctification and what we might term "the visible aspects of the church." With the Constantinian shift these issues were given less attention. When the church is everyone, the visible expression of the church and the sanctifying characteristics of Christian existence become less important. The change in context shifted the focus, and attention to the areas of ecclesiology, Christian ethics and sanctification diminished. With the incorporation of everyone into the church, the context called for other areas of theology to be developed instead. The Constantinian shift, in all likelihood, influenced doctrinal development in this way.

That these related areas are beginning to appear again has to do with the fact that the church in the West is standing at the end of the Constantinian era, and it is now becoming evident that these areas of doctrine were not properly developed. Historical events led to some parts of Christian doctrine not being worked on, but current contextual changes might bring these areas to the forefront of theology again.

Ecclesiology has traditionally been linked to teaching on the Holy Spirit (pneumatology), and the Holy Spirit has, in the history of theology, been the person of the Trinity given the least attention.[9] With the end of the Constantinian era it seems like there are areas, which are again about to be developed, thus advancing a long overdue development of Christian doctrine in the West.

---

9. "Pneumatology was for long a neglected doctrine in Western Christianity." See Wainwright, "Holy Spirit," 289.

If the church in the West is in the process of leaving the Constantinian era, does this mean that the church is now facing a time of turmoil and suffering? Since there are persecuted churches in many parts of the world right now, and God's church is always connected across any national borders, it is a fact that also the church in the West is suffering. However, for the church in the West, the change in context will not necessarily entail suffering or a bleak future as such. As Stanley Hauerwas has pointed out, it is exactly when the church has nothing to lose that it can dare be adventurous. It is in the situation, where there is no way that God makes a way. The story of the Israelites facing the Red Sea is just one instance of how, throughout the biblical story, this feature of God's way of acting is made known. It is when everything looks bleak and without a future that God makes a way. The crucifixion was the darkest moment in the history of the world. However, it was followed by a resurrection and something completely new. The church in the West is losing members and, in some countries, though certainly not everywhere, the church is facing persecution. Nevertheless, God makes a way where there is no way, and that is the most secure ground onto which the church in the West and everywhere can cast its anchor of hope.

Bibliography

Anisfeld, Moshe. "Why Was Moses Barred from Leading the People into the Promised Land? A Psychotheological Answer." *Jewish Bible Quarterly* 39 (2011) 211–20.
Arbesman, Samuel. "The Return of History at Long Timescales." *Wired*, January 29, 2014. http://www.wired.com/wiredscience/2014/01/return-of-history-long-timescales/.
Armitage, David, and Joanna Guldi. "A Return of the *Longue Durée*: An Anglo-American Perspective." *Annales. Histoire, Sciences sociales* (English ed. preview) 69 (2014) 1–45.
———. "What's the Big Idea? Intellectual History and the Longue Durée." *History of European Ideas* 38 (2012) 493–507.
Augustine. *Augustine of Hippo: Selected Writings*. Edited by Mary T. Clark. New York: Paulist, 1984.
———. *La cité de Dieu*. Translated by Gustave Combès. 4th ed. Oeuvres de Saint Augustin. Paris: Desclée de Brouwer, 1959.
———. *The City of God*. Translated by Marcus Dods. New York: Random House, 2000.
———. *The City of God Against the Pagans*. Translated by Robert W. Dyson. Cambridge: Cambridge University Press, 1998.
———. *The City of God Against the Pagans*. Bks. 12–15. Translated by Philip Levine. Edited by Jeffrey Henderson. Loeb Classical Library 4. Cambridge: Harvard University Press, 2002.
———. *Concerning the City of God Against the Pagans*. Translated by Henry Bettenson. London: Penguin, 1984.
———. *The Retractions*. Translated by Mary Inez Bogan. Fathers of the Church 60. New York: Catholic University of America Press, 2010.
Avery, William T. "The 'Adoratio Purpurae' and the Importance of the Imperial Purple in the Fourth Century of the Christian Era." *Memoirs of the American Academy in Rome* 17 (1940) 66–80.
Bainton, Roland Herbert. *Christian Attitudes toward War and Peace: A Historical Survey and Critical Re-evaluation*. New York: Abingdon, 1960.
Bammel, Caroline P. "Augustine, Origen and the Exegesis of St. Paul." *Augustinianum* 32 (1992) 341–68.
Barnes, Timothy D. *Constantine and Eusebius*. Cambridge: Harvard University Press, 1981.
———. *Constantine: Dynasty, Religion and Power in the Later Roman Empire*. Chichester, UK: Wiley-Blackwell, 2011.
———. "Panegyric, History and Hagiography in Eusebius' *Life of Constantine*." In *The Making of Orthodoxy: Essays in Honour of Henry Chadwick*, edited by Rowan Williams, 94–123. New York: Cambridge University Press, 1989.

Bibliography

Barth, Karl. *Fragments Grave and Gay*. London: Collins, 1971.
Bender, Harold Stauffer. "The Anabaptist Vision." In *The Recovery of the Anabaptist Vision*, edited by Guy F. Hershberger, 29–56. Scottdale, PA: Herald, 1957.
Bevans, Stephen B. *Models of Contextual Theology*. Faith and Cultures Series. Maryknoll: Orbis, 2002.
Bloch, Marc. *The Historian's Craft*. Translated by Peter Putnam. New York: Vintage, 1953.
Bosch, David Jacobus. *Transforming Mission: Paradigm Shifts in Theology of Mission*. Maryknoll: Orbis, 1991.
Braudel, Fernand. "Histoire et Sciences sociales: La longue durée." *Annales. Économies, Sociétés, Civilisations* 13 (1958) 725–53.
Bretherton, Luke. *Christianity and Contemporary Politics: The Conditions and Possibilities of Faithful Witness*. Chichester, UK: Wiley-Blackwell, 2010.
Burckhardt, Jacob. *The Age of Constantine the Great*. Translated by Moses Hadas. Berkeley: University of California Press, 2011.
Burguière, André. *The Annales School: An Intellectual History*. Translated by Jane Marie Todd. Ithaca, NY: Cornell University Press, 2009.
Cameron, Averil. *Christianity and the Rhetoric of Empire: The Development of Christian Discourse*. Los Angeles: University of California Press, 1991.
———. "Eusebius' *Vita Constantini* and the Construction of Constantine." In *Portraits: Biographical Representation in the Greek and Latin Literature of the Roman Empire*, edited by M. J. Edwards and Simon Swain, 145–74. New York: Oxford University Press, 1997.
Cameron, Averil, and Stuart George Hall. *Introduction and Commentaries to "Life of Constantine."* Clarendon Ancient History Series. New York: Oxford University Press, 1999.
Cavanaugh, William T. "From One City to Two: Christian Reimagining of Political Space." *Political Theology* 7 (2006) 299–321.
———. *Theopolitical Imagination: Christian Practices of Space and Time*. Edinburgh: T. & T. Clark, 2003.
Chesnut, Glenn F. "Eusebius, Augustine, Orosius, and the Later Patristic and Medieval Christian Historians." In *Eusebius, Christianity, and Judaism*, edited by Harold W. Attridge and Gohei Hata, 687–713. Detroit: Wayne State University Press, 1992.
———. "The Pattern of the Past: Augustine's Debate with Eusebius and Sallust." In *Our Common History as Christians: Essays in Honor of Albert C. Outler*, edited by John Deschner, 351–77. New York: Oxford University Press, 1975.
Christian, David. "The Return of Universal History." *History and Theory* 49 (2010) 6–27.
Collier, Charles Mayo. "A Nonviolent Augustinianism? History and Politics in the Theologies of St. Augustine and John Howard Yoder." PhD diss., Duke University, 2008.
Couenhoven, Jesse. "St. Augustine's Doctrine of Original Sin." *Augustinian Studies* 36 (2005) 359–96.
Cranmer, Frank, and Javier García Oliva. "Church-State Relationships: An Overview." *Law & Justice: The Christian Law Review* 162 (2009) 4–17.
Dagron, Gilbert. *Emperor and Priest: The Imperial Office in Byzantium*. Translated by Jean Birrell. Cambridge: Cambridge University Press, 2003.
Davis, Ellen F., and Richard B. Hays, eds. *The Art of Reading Scripture*. Grand Rapids: Eerdmans, 2003.
De La Torre, Miguel A. *Reading the Bible from the Margins*. Maryknoll: Orbis, 2002.

Bibliography

Donnelly, Dorothy F., and Mark A. Sherman. *Augustine's De Civitate Dei: An Annotated Bibliography of Modern Criticism, 1960–1990.* New York: Peter Lang, 1991.

Drake, Harold Allen. *Constantine and the Bishops: The Politics of Intolerance.* Baltimore: Johns Hopkins University Press, 2000.

Dreher, Rod. *The Benedict Option: A Strategy for Christians in a Post-Christian Nation.* New York: Sentinel, 2017.

Dula, Peter, and Chris K. Huebner, eds. *The New Yoder.* Eugene, OR: Cascad, 2010.

Dumont, Louis. *Essays on Individualism: Modern Ideology in Anthropological Perspective.* Chicago: University of Chicago Press, 1986.

Dyck, Cornelius J. *An Introduction to Mennonite History: A Popular History of the Anabaptists and the Mennonites.* 3rd ed. Mennonite History. Scottdale, PA: Herald, 1993.

East, Bradley. "On Being a Scholar of John Howard Yoder without Ignoring or Omitting His Mistreatment of Women." *Resident Theology* (blog), September 24, 2013. http://resident-theology.blogspot.com/2013/09/on-being-scholar-of-john-howard-yoder.html

Estep, William Roscoe. *The Anabaptist Story: An Introduction to Sixteenth-Century Anabaptism.* Grand Rapids: Eerdmans, 1996.

Eusebius. *Eusebius Werke.* 1/1. Translated by Friedhelm Winkelmann. Berlin: Akademie-Verlag, 1991.

———. *Eusebius Werke Erster Band. Über das Leben Constantins; Constantins Rede an die heilige Versammlung; Tricennatsrede an Constantin.* Translated by Ivar August Heikel. Leipzig: Hinrichs, 1902.

———. *The History of the Church.* Translated by Arthur Cushman McGiffert. Stilwell, KS: Digireads, 2005.

———. *Life of Constantine.* Translated by Averil Cameron and Stuart George Hall. Clarendon Ancient History Series. New York: Oxford University Press, 1999.

———. *Oration in Praise of Constantine / De Laudibus Constantini.* Edited by Philip Schaff and Henry Wace. Nicene and Post-Nicene Fathers 1. Grand Rapids: Eerdmans, 1979.

Field, Lester L. *Liberty, Dominion, and the Two Swords: On the Origins of Western Political Theology (180–398).* Notre Dame: University of Notre Dame Press, 1998.

Finger, Thomas N. "Anabaptism and Eastern Orthodoxy: Some Unexpected Similarities?" *Journal of Ecumenical Studies* 31 (1994) 67–91.

Fowden, Garth. "The Last Days of Constantine: Oppositional Versions and Their Influence." *Journal of Roman Studies* 84 (1994) 146–70.

Frei, Hans W. *The Eclipse of Biblical Narrative: A Study in Eighteenth and Nineteenth Century Hermeneutics.* New Haven: Yale University Press, 1974.

Frend, William Hugh C. Review of *Monotheismus als politisches Problem? Erik Peterson und die Kritik der politischen Theologie*, edited by A. Schindler. *Journal of Ecclesiastical History* 32 (1981) 251–52.

Fukuyama, Francis. *The End of History and the Last Man.* London: Hamish Hamilton, 1992.

Goossen, Rachel Waltner. "'Defanging the Beast': Mennonite Responses to John Howard Yoder's Sexual Abuse." *Mennonite Quarterly Review* 89 (2015) 7–80.

Greenslade, Stanley L. *Church and State from Constantine to Theodosius.* London: SCM, 1954.

Guroian, Vigen. *Incarnate Love: Essays in Orthodox Ethics.* Notre Dame: University of Notre Dame Press, 1987.

Bibliography

Hauerwas, Stanley. "In Defence of 'Our Respectable Culture': Trying to Make Sense of John Howard Yoder's Sexual Abuse." ABC Religion & Ethics, October 18, 2017. http://www.abc.net.au/religion/articles/2017/10/18/4751367.htm

———. *In Good Company: The Church as Polis*. Notre Dame: University of Notre Dame Press, 1995.

———. *Matthew*. Brazos Theological Commentary on the Bible. Grand Rapids: Brazos, 2006.

Hauerwas, Stanley, and William H. Willimon. *Resident Aliens: Life in the Christian Colony*. Nashville: Abingdon, 1989.

Hays, Richard B. *The Moral Vision of the New Testament: A Contemporary Introduction to New Testament Ethics*. San Francisco: HarperCollins, 1996.

Hollenbach, David. *The Common Good and Christian Ethics*. New Studies in Christian Ethics. New York: Cambridge University Press, 2002.

Hollerich, Michael J. "Religion and Politics in the Writings of Eusebius: Reassessing the First 'Court Theologian.'" *Church History* 59 (1990) 309–25.

Holsclaw, Geoffrey. "Transcending Subjects: Hegel after Augustine, an Essay on Political Theology." PhD diss., Marquette University, 2013.

Huebner, Chris K., and Stanley Hauerwas. *A Precarious Peace: Yoderian Explorations on Theology, Knowledge, and Identity*. Waterloo, ON: Herald, 2006.

Hunter-Bowman, Janna L. "The Opportunity Stanley Hauerwas Missed." *Christian Century*, October 26, 2017. https://www.christiancentury.org/blog-post/guest-post/opportunity-stanley-hauerwas-missed

Iggers, Georg G. "The Image of Ranke in American and German Historical Thought." *History and Theory* 2 (1962) 17–40.

———. Review of *The Annales School: An Intellectual History*, by André Burguière. *Enterprise & Society* 13 (2012) 221–24.

Inowlocki, Sabrina, and Claudio Zamagni, eds. *Reconsidering Eusebius: Collected Papers on Literary, Historical, and Theological Issues*. Supplements to Vigiliae Christianae. Leiden: Brill, 2011.

Jameson, Fredric. *Postmodernism; or, The Cultural Logic of Late Capitalism*. Durham, NC: Duke University Press, 1991.

Jenson, Robert W. "The Church and the Sacraments." In *The Cambridge Companion to Christian Doctrine*, edited by Colin E. Gunton, 207–25. Cambridge: Cambridge University Press, 1997.

Johnson, Aaron P., and Jeremy M. Schott. *Eusebius of Caesarea: Tradition and Innovations*. Cambridge: Harvard University Press, 2013.

Kelsey, David H. *Eccentric Existence: A Theological Anthropology*. 2 vols. Louisville: Westminster John Knox, 2009.

Kierkegaard, Søren. *Søren Kierkegaard's Journals and Papers*. Vol. 1, A–E. Translated by Howard V. Hong and Edna H. Hong. Bloomington: Indiana University Press, 1967.

———. *Søren Kierkegaards skrifter*. Vol. 25. Edited by Niels Jørgen Cappelørn et al. Copenhagen: Gads Forlag, 1997.

Kreider, Alan. "'Converted' but Not Baptized: Peter Leithart's Constantine Project." In *Constantine Revisited: Leithart, Yoder, and the Constantinian Debate*, edited by John D. Roth, 25–67. Eugene, OR: Pickwick, 2013.

Langan, John. "The Elements of St. Augustine's Just War Theory." *Journal of Religious Ethics* 12 (1984) 19–38.

Bibliography

Lee, Gregory W. "Republics and Their Loves: Rereading City of God 19." *Modern Theology* 27 (2011) 553–81.

Leithart, Peter J. *Defending Constantine: The Twilight of an Empire and the Dawn of Christendom*. Downers Grove: IVP Academic, 2010.

———. *Gratitude: An Intellectual History*. Waco, TX: Baylor University Press, 2014.

LeMasters, Philip. *The Import of Eschatology in John Howard Yoder's Critique of Constantinianism*. San Francisco: Mellen Research University Press, 1992.

Lewis, Charlton, and Charles Thomas Short. *A Latin Dictionary*. 6th ed. New York: Oxford University Press, 1998.

Liddell, Henry George, and Robert F. Scott. *A Greek-English Lexicon: Compiled by Henry George Liddell and Robert Scott*. 9th ed. Oxford: Clarendon, 1940.

Lindbeck, George A. *The Nature of Doctrine: Religion and Theology in a Postliberal Age*. Philadelphia: Westminster, 1984.

Luther, Martin. *Von der babylonischen Gefangenschaft der Kirche*. Edited by Kurt Aland. 2nd ed. Luther Deutsch: Die Werke Martin Luthers in neuer Auswahl für die Gegenwart. Band 2. Göttingen: Vandenhoeck & Ruprecht, 1981.

MacCormack, Sabine G. *Art and Ceremony in Late Antiquity*. Transformation of the Classical Heritage. Berkeley: University of California Press, 1981.

MacCulloch, Diarmaid. *A History of Christianity: The First Three Thousand Years*. New York: Allen Lane, 2009.

Mantovani, Mauro. *Bellum Iustum: Die Idee des gerechten Krieges in der römischen Kaiserzeit*. Bern: Peter Lang, 1990.

Markus, Robert A. *Christianity and the Secular*. Notre Dame: University of Notre Dame Press, 2006.

———. *Saeculum: History and Society in the Theology of St. Augustine*. Cambridge: Cambridge University Press, 1970.

———. "*Tempora Christiana* Revisited." In *Augustine and His Critiques: Essays in Honor of Gerald Bonner*, edited by Robert Dodaro and George Lawless, 201–13. London: Routledge, 2000.

Martens, Paul Henry. *The Heterodox Yoder*. Eugene, OR: Cascade, 2012.

Martinson, Mattias. "Postliberal Theology." In *Encyclopedia of Sciences and Religions*, edited by Anne Runehov and Lluis Oviedo, 1817–23. Dordrecht: Springer Verlag, 2013.

Mattox, John Mark. *St. Augustine and the Theory of Just War*. London: Continuum International, 2006.

Mayer, Cornelius. *Augustinus-Lexicon*. Edited by Andreas E. J. Grote. Vol. 3. Basel: Schwabe, 2010.

Milbank, John. *Theology and Social Theory: Beyond Secular Reason*. Oxford: Blackwell, 2006.

Nation, Mark Theissen. "John Howard Yoder: Mennonite, Evangelical, Catholic." *Mennonite Quately Review* 76 (2003) 357–70.

———. *John Howard Yoder: Mennonite Patience, Evangelical Witness, Catholic Convictions*. Grand Rapids: Eerdmans, 2006.

Newbigin, Lesslie. *The Gospel in a Pluralist Society*. Grand Rapids: Eerdmans, 1989.

Newman, John Henry. *An Essay on the Development of Christian Doctrine*. 2nd ed. London: Toovey, 1846.

Nichols, Aidan. "'Non tali auxilio': John Milbank's Suasion to Orthodoxy." *New Blackfriars* 73 (1992) 326–32.

Bibliography

Nikolajsen, Jeppe Bach. *The Distinctive Identity of the Church: A Constructive Study of the Post-Christendom Theologies of Lesslie Newbigin and John Howard Yoder*. Eugene, OR: Pickwick, 2015.

———. "Menighedens liv med Bibelen: Menigheden som et hermeneutisk fællesskab ifølge John Howard Yoder." *Dansk Tidsskrift for Teologi og Kirke* 42 (2015) 5–18.

———. "Missional Folk Church? A Discussion of Hans Raun Iversen's Understanding of the Danish Folk Church as a Missional Church." *Swedish Missiological Themes* 100 (2012) 23–36.

———. "Redefining the Identity of the Church: A Constructive Study of the Post-Christendom Theologies of Lesslie Newbigin and John Howard Yoder." PhD diss., MF Norwegian School of Theology, Oslo, 2010.

O'Daly, Gerard J. P. *Augustine's City of God: A Reader's Guide*. New York: Oxford University Press, 1999.

O'Donnell, James J. "Augustine, *City of God*." 1983. Unpublished conference paper. Available at http://www9.georgetown.edu/faculty/jod/augustine/civ.html

O'Donovan, Oliver. *The Desire of the Nations: Rediscovering the Roots of Political Theology*. Cambridge: Cambridge University Press, 1996.

———. "The Political Thought of City of God 19." In *Bonds of Imperfection: Christian Politics, Past and Present*, edited by Joan Lockwood O'Donovan and Oliver O'Donovan, 48–72. Grand Rapids: Eerdmans, 2004.

Oppenheimer, Mark. "A Theologian's Influence, and Stained Past, Live On." *New York Times*, October 12, 2013.

Paddison, Angus. Review of *To See History Doxologically: History and Holiness in John Howard Yoder's Ecclesiology*, by J. Alexander Sider. *Studies in Christian Ethics* 25 (2012) 388–90.

Pannenberg, Wolfhart. *Systematische Theologie*. 3 vols. Vol. 3. Göttingen: Vandenhoeck und Ruprecht, 1993.

Penner, Reuben J. "The Rhetoric of God in History: Eusebius of Caesarea's Political Theology in His 'Panegyric to Constantine.'" MA thesis, Dalhousie University, Halifax, Nova Scotia, 2008.

Peterson, Erik. *Der Monotheismus als politisches Problem: Ein Beitrag zur Geschichte der politischen Theologie im Imperium Romanum*. Leipzig: Jakob Hegner Verlag, 1935.

Phillips, Jonathan. *The Fourth Crusade and the Sack of Constantinople*. New York: Viking, 2004.

Pollmann, Karla F. L. Review of *Augustine's City of God: A Reader's Guide*, by Gerard O'Daly. *Church History: Studies in Christianity and Culture* 68 (1999) 970–71.

Rasmusson, Arne. *The Church as Polis: From Political Theology to Theological Politics as Exemplified by Jürgen Moltmann and Stanley Hauerwas*. Notre Dame: University of Notre Dame Press, 1995.

Ratzinger, Joseph. *Volk und Haus Gottes in Augustins Lehre von der Kirche*. Münchener Theologische Studien. Munich: Karl Zink Verlag, 1954.

Roth, John D., ed. *Constantine Revisited: Leithart, Yoder, and the Constantinian Debate*. Eugene, OR: Pickwick, 2013.

Ruhbach, Gerhard. "Die politische Theologie Eusebs von Caesarea." In *Die Kirche angesichts der konstantinischen Wende*, edited by Gerhard Ruhbach, 236–58. Darmstadt, Germany: Wissenschaftliche Buchgesellschaft, 1976.

Sanders, E. P. *Paul, the Law, and the Jewish People*. Philadelphia: Fortress, 1983.

Bibliography

Scarsella, Hilary. "Not Making Sense: Why Stanley Hauerwas's Response to Yoder's Sexual Abuse Misses the Mark." ABC Religion & Ethics, November 30, 2017. http://www.abc.net.au/religion/articles/2017/11/30/4774014.htm.

Schlabach, Gerald W. "The Christian Witness in the Earthly City: John H. Yoder as Augustinian Interlocutor." Paper presented at the conference "Assessing the Theological Legacy of John Howard Yoder," University of Notre Dame, March 7, 2002.

———. "Deuteronomic or Constantinian: What Is the Most Basic Problem for Christian Social Ethics?" In *The Wisdom of the Cross: Essays in Honor of John Howard Yoder*, edited by Stanley Hauerwas et al., 449-71. Grand Rapids: Eerdmans, 1999.

Schmitt, Carl. *Politische Theologie: Vier Kapitel zur Lehre von der Souveränität*. Munich: Duncker u. Humblot, 1922.

Seston, William. "Constantine as a 'Bishop.'" *Journal of Roman Studies* 37 (1947) 127-31.

Sider, J. Alexander. "Constantinianism Before and After Nicea." In *A Mind Patient and Untamed: Assessing John Howard Yoder's Contributions to Theology, Ethics, and Peacemaking*, edited by Ben C. Ollenburger and Gayle Gerber Koontz, 126-44. Scottdale, PA: Herald, 2004.

———. *To See History Doxologically: History and Holiness in John Howard Yoder's Ecclesiology*. Grand Rapids: Eerdmans, 2011.

Sirinelli, Jean. *Les vues historiques d'Eusèbe de Césarée durant la période prénicéenne*. Publications de la Section de Langues et Littératures 10. Dakar, Senegal: Université de Dakar, 1961.

Sjørup, Lene. "Jesus med og uden bryster." *Præsteforeningens Blad* 103 (2013) 550-54.

Stark, Rodney. *The Rise of Christianity: A Sociologist Reconsiders History*. Princeton: Princeton University Press, 1996.

Stayer, James M., et al. "From Monogenesis to Polygenesis: The Historical Discussion of Anabaptist Origins." *Mennonite Quarterly Review* 49 (1975) 83-121.

Stendahl, Krister. "The Apostle Paul and the Introspective Conscience of the West." *Harvard Theological Review* 56 (1963) 199-215.

Stephenson, Paul. *Constantine: Roman Emperor, Christian Victor*. New York: Overlook, 2010.

Swedberg, Richard. *The Max Weber Dictionary: Key Words and Central Concepts*. Stanford: Stanford Social Sciences, 2005.

Tanner, Kathryn. *Theories of Culture: A New Agenda for Theology*. Minneapolis: Fortress, 1997.

Tassi, Adriano. *Hegel a Berna: Le premesse di un sistema*. Soveria Mannelli, Italy: Rubbettino, 2003.

Templin, J. Alton. "Adam Pastor: Anti-Trinitarian Anabaptist." *Iliff Review* 24 (1967) 25-31.

Thompson, Glen L. "From Sinner to Saint? Seeking a Consistent Constantine." In *Rethinking Constantine: History, Theology, and Legacy*, edited by Edward L. Smither, 5-25. Eugene, OR: Pickwick, 2014.

Tran, Jonathan. "*Defending Constantine* Taken Seriously." In *Constantine Revisited: Leithart, Yoder, and the Constantinian Debate*, edited by John D. Roth, 124-32. Eugene, OR: Pickwick, 2013.

Wainwright, Geoffrey. "The Holy Spirit." In *The Cambridge Companion to Christian Doctrine*, edited by Colin E. Gunton, 273-96. Cambridge: Cambridge University Press. 1997.

Bibliography

Ward, Graham. "Questioning God." In *Questioning God*, edited by John D. Caputo et al., 274–90. Bloomington: Indiana University Press, 2001.

Westerholm, Stephen. *Israel's Law and the Church's Faith: Paul and His Recent Interpreters*. Grand Rapids: Eerdmans, 1988.

Williams, Rowan. "Politics and the Soul: A Reading of the *City of God*." In *An Eerdmans Reader in Contemporary Political Theology*, edited by William T. Cavanaugh et al., 731–49. Grand Rapids: Eerdmans, 2012.

Yoder, John Howard. *Anabaptism and Reformation in Switzerland: An Historical and Theological Analysis of the Dialogues between Anabaptists and Reformers*. Translated by Arnold Snyder and David Carl Stassen. Kitchener, ON: Pandora, 2004.

———. *Christian Attitudes to War, Peace, and Revolution*. Edited by Andy Alexis-Baker and Theodore J. Koontz. Grand Rapids: Brazos, 2009.

———. *Christian Attitudes to War, Peace, and Revolution: A Companion to Bainton*. Elkhart, IN: Goshen Biblical Seminary, 1983.

———. "Historiography as a Ministry to Renewal." *Brethren Life and Thought* 42 (1997) 216–28.

———. "The Original Revolution." In *The Original Revolution: Essays on Christian Pacifism*. Scottdale, PA: Herald, 1972.

———. *The Politics of Jesus: Vicit Agnus Noster*. Grand Rapids: Eerdmans, 1972.

———. *Die Politik Jesu*. Translated by Wolfgang Krauss. Schwarzenfeld, Germany: Neufeld, 2012.

———. *The Priestly Kingdom: Social Ethics as Gospel*. Notre Dame: University of Notre Dame Press, 1984.

———. *The Royal Priesthood: Essays Ecclesiological and Ecumenical*. Edited by Michael G. Cartwright. Scottdale, PA: Herald, 1998.

———. *Täufertum und Reformation in der Schweiz: Die Gespräche zwischen Täufern und Reformatoren 1523–1538*. Karlsruhe, Germany: H. Schneider Verlag, 1962.

———. "The Use of the Bible in Theology." In *The Use of the Bible in Theology: Evangelical Options*, edited by Robert K. Johnston, 103–20. Atlanta: Westminster John Knox, 1985.